Apress Pocket Guides

Apress Pocket Guides present concise summaries of cutting-edge developments and working practices throughout the tech industry. Shorter in length, books in this series aims to deliver quick-to-read guides that are easy to absorb, perfect for the time-poor professional.

This series covers the full spectrum of topics relevant to the modern industry, from security, AI, machine learning, cloud computing, web development, product design, to programming techniques and business topics too.

Typical topics might include:

- A concise guide to a particular topic, method, function or framework

- Professional best practices and industry trends

- A snapshot of a hot or emerging topic

- Industry case studies

- Concise presentations of core concepts suited for students and those interested in entering the tech industry

- Short reference guides outlining 'need-to-know' concepts and practices.

More information about this series at https://link.springer.com/bookseries/17385.

Creational Design Patterns in Java

Designing Flexible, Scalable, and Reliable Software

Vaskaran Sarcar

Apress®

Creational Design Patterns in Java: Designing Flexible, Scalable, and Reliable Software

Vaskaran Sarcar 🄳
Kolkata, West Bengal, India

ISBN-13 (pbk): 979-8-8688-2313-8 ISBN-13 (electronic): 979-8-8688-2314-5
https://doi.org/10.1007/979-8-8688-2314-5

Managing Director, Apress Media LLC: Welmoed Spahr
Acquisitions Editor: Melissa Duffy
Coordinating Editor: Gryffin Winkler

Cover designed by eStudioCalamar

Distributed to the book trade worldwide by Springer Science+Business Media New York, 1 New York Plaza, New York, NY 10004. Phone 1-800-SPRINGER, fax (201) 348-4505, e-mail orders-ny@springer-sbm.com, or visit www.springeronline.com. Apress Media, LLC is a Delaware LLC and the sole member (owner) is Springer Science + Business Media Finance Inc (SSBM Finance Inc). SSBM Finance Inc is a **Delaware** corporation.

For information on translations, please e-mail booktranslations@springernature.com; for reprint, paperback, or audio rights, please e-mail bookpermissions@springernature.com.

Apress titles may be purchased in bulk for academic, corporate, or promotional use. eBook versions and licenses are also available for most titles. For more information, reference our Print and eBook Bulk Sales web page at http://www.apress.com/bulk-sales.

Any source code or other supplementary material referenced by the author in this book is available to readers on GitHub (https://github.com/Apress/Creational-Design-Patterns-in-Java). For more detailed information, please visit https://www.apress.com/gp/services/source-code.

If disposing of this product, please recycle the paper

Table of Contents

About the Author

 **Vaskaran Sarcar** brings a unique blend of academic rigor and industry leadership to his technical writing. A National GATE Scholar, Vaskaran has leveraged over 18 years of professional experience in teaching, software development, and programming to become an established author. His portfolio includes multiple editions of well-received titles such as *Java Design Patterns* and *Design Patterns in C#*, with his book *Interactive C#* also translated into Japanese. Before focusing on full-time authorship, he spent a decade as a Senior Software Engineer and Team Lead at HP India's PPS R&D Hub, where he specialized in designing automation test frameworks and resolving critical defects. Vaskaran is passionate about transforming complex ideas into accessible knowledge for learners worldwide. You can find his work on Amazon[1] and Springer.[2] You can connect with him on LinkedIn.[3]

---

[1] https://www.amazon.com/author/vaskaran_sarcar

[2] https://link.springer.com/search?newsearch=true&query=vaskaran+sarcar&content-type=book&dateFrom=&dateTo=&sortBy=newestFirst

[3] https://www.linkedin.com/in/vaskaransarcar

About the Technical Reviewer

Manuel Jordan Elera is an autodidactic developer and researcher who enjoys learning new technologies for his own experiments and creating new integrations. Manuel won the Springy Award 2013 Community Champion and Spring Champion. In his little free time, he reads the Bible and composes music on his guitar. Manuel is known as dr_pompeii. He has tech-reviewed numerous books, including *Pro Spring MVC with WebFlux* (Apress, 2020), *Pro Spring Boot 2* (Apress, 2019), *Rapid Java Persistence and Microservices* (Apress, 2019), *Java Language Features* (Apress, 2018), *Spring Boot 2 Recipes* (Apress, 2018), and *Java APIs, Extensions and Libraries* (Apress, 2018). You can read his detailed tutorials on Spring technologies and contact him through his blog at www.manueljordanelera.blogspot.com. You can follow Manuel on his Twitter account, @dr_pompeii.

Acknowledgments

At first, I thank the Almighty. I believe that I was able to complete this book with HIS blessings. I extend my deepest gratitude and thanks to the following people.

Manuel Jordan Elera—Manuel is the technical reviewer of this book. I sincerely thank him for his thorough reviews, insightful suggestions, and thoughtful improvement ideas, all of which have significantly enhanced the quality of this work.

Melissa and the Apress team—I sincerely thank each of you for giving me another opportunity to work with you.

Nirmal, copy editor (Tusca Omangay), and production team members (Jagathesan and Vinoth)—Thanks to each of you for your exceptional support in beautifying my work. Your efforts are extraordinary.

Finally, I thank the members of various online communities—such as the Oracle Java Community, Reddit (r/Java), and Stack Overflow—who generously share their knowledge in many forms. I also extend my gratitude to everyone who has directly or indirectly contributed to this work.

Introduction

Welcome to your journey through *Creational Design Patterns in Java*. The concepts of design patterns are universal, and applying them in Java opens new opportunities for writing flexible, maintainable, and reusable code.

You probably know that the design patterns became popular through the Gang of Four's (GoF) classic book, *Design Patterns: Elements of Reusable Object-Oriented Software* (Addison-Wesley, 1994). The GoF book was published long before and focused on C++. On the contrary, since its birth in 1995, Java has been enriched with new features, and it is quite mature now. So, you may think: Do I still need these patterns?

First, let me tell you that many of these patterns form the foundation of today's programming practices. Next, design patterns require neither unusual language features nor amazing programming tricks to surprise others. If a supporting feature is not available, you may need to put some extra effort into achieving long-term flexibility and reusability. So, it's no surprise that the GoF book remains a bestseller on Amazon.

The classical GoF book cataloged 23 patterns into three categories—Creational, Structural, and Behavioral. They grouped five patterns: Abstract Factory, Factory Method, Prototype, Builder, and Singleton under the creational patterns. The creational patterns are about the creation of objects (yes, though the singleton restricts the number of objects, it is still creational). At a high level, these patterns abstract the instantiation process and help you make the systems independent from how their objects are composed, created, and represented. To illustrate, while implementing these patterns, you normally ask: "Where should I place the **'new'** keyword in my application?" This decision can determine the degree of coupling of your classes.

Over the period, the Abstract Factory became peripheral (see "Design Patterns 15 Years Later: An Interview with Erich Gamma, Richard Helm, and Ralph Johnson," InformIT[1]). So, I did not discuss this pattern in this pocketbook. Instead, I included the discussion on the Dependency Injection (DI) pattern (instead of considering it as a single pattern, some developers and authors consider DI as a set of patterns and principles). It is interesting to note that later, one of the GoF authors, Ralph Johnson, acknowledged that the name of this pattern came out after their book was published. He also stated that they'd like to include DI in the second edition of their book (see JDD2015 – Twenty-one Years of Design Patterns (Ralph Johnson), YouTube[2]). This is why **this pocketbook covers four GoF patterns and one non-GoF pattern.**

How Is the Book Organized?

To give you an idea about the contents of this book, let me summarize the contents of the book:

Chapter 1 explains the need for a factory. It demystifies the **Simple Factory** idiom, which is not strictly a GoF pattern, and ends with a **Factory Method** implementation.

Chapter 2 discusses the **Singleton** pattern with four different implementations.

Chapter 3 includes three different implementations to explain different variations of the **Builder** pattern.

Chapter 4 shows two different **Prototype** pattern implementations and points out the differences between a shallow copy and a deep copy. This chapter also compares the Prototype and Factory Method patterns.

---

[1] https://www.informit.com/articles/article.aspx?p=1404056&lang=en

[2] https://www.youtube.com/watch?v=BfHJo_aYj3g

Additionally, a sample "Prototype implementation using a copy constructor" is provided for reference, which is not shown in the book but can be downloaded from the publisher's website.

Chapter 5 explains the **Dependency Injection** pattern with six different implementations and compares the techniques.

Appendix A discusses the alternative implementations and potential improvements for some of the implementations in this book.

Appendix B suggests additional resources for further reading.

Appendix C lists my other books for your reference.

You can enjoy learning when you analyze these implementations and ask questions (about the doubts). So, throughout this book, you will see many "Q&A Sessions." Each question in these Q&A sessions is marked with **Q<chapter_no>.<Question_no>**. For example, **Q3.2** means question number 2 of Chapter 3. These are presented to make your future learning easier and enjoyable, but most importantly, they make you confident as a developer.

You can download all the book's source code from the publisher's website (https://github.com/Apress/Creational-Design-Patterns-in-Java).

Prerequisite Knowledge

I expect you to be familiar with Java and how to compile or run a Java application. In short, the target readers of this book are those who have an idea about the pure object-oriented concepts like polymorphism, inheritance, abstraction, and encapsulation. While implementing the patterns, I want you to make the most out of Java by harnessing the power of both object-oriented programming (OOP) and functional programming (FP).

Who This Book Is For

You can read this book if the answer is "yes" to the following questions:

- Are you familiar with Java and basic object-oriented concepts like polymorphism, inheritance, abstraction, and encapsulation?

- Do you know how to set up your coding environment?

- Do you want to explore the creational design patterns in Java step-by-step?

You probably shouldn't read this book if the answer is "yes" to any of the following questions:

- While writing this book, I used Eclipse IDE in a Windows 11 environment. Are you not comfortable exploring the patterns using this setup?

- "I am already confident about GoF design patterns and other patterns that you mentioned earlier. I am searching for other patterns." Is this statement true for you?

Guidelines for Using This Book

Here are some suggestions so that you can get the most out of this book:

Sequential reading of these chapters can help you learn faster. This is because some useful and related topics may have already been discussed in a previous chapter, and I have not repeated those discussions in the later chapters.

The programs in this book should give you the expected output in the upcoming versions of Java as well. Though I believe that these results should not vary in other environments, you know the nature of software: it is naughty! So, I recommend that if you want to see the same output, it will be better if you can mimic the same environment.

Useful Software

During the development of this book, software updates kept coming, and I also kept updating my tools accordingly. By the time I completed the draft, I was using **Java 24.0.2** and **Eclipse 202503 (4.35.0, Build id: 202503060812)**. You can surely predict that version updates will come continuously, but these version details should not matter much to you because I have focused on the fundamental constructs of Java. So, I believe that these programs should execute smoothly in the upcoming versions of Java/Eclipse as well. You can download Eclipse from the official link, https:// www.eclipse.org/downloads/, and expect to see the following (Figure 1).

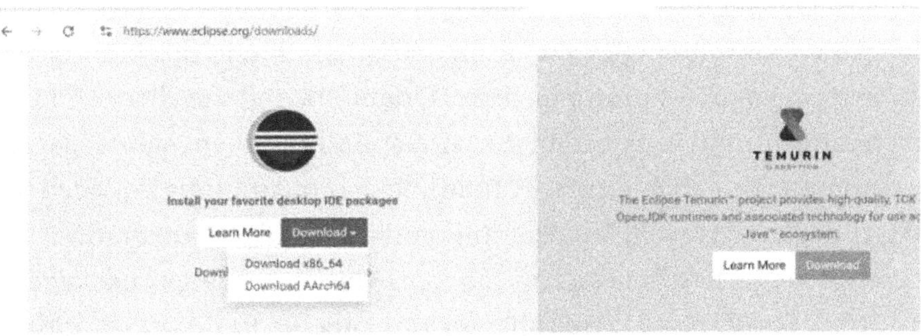

Figure 1. *Download link for Eclipse IDE*

Note   At the time of this writing, this link works fine, and the information is correct. However, the link and policies may change in the future. The same comment applies to all the mentioned links in this book.

Before coding, I often use a pen/pencil, markers, and a whiteboard to draft ideas. However, I used **Eclipse Papyrus** (EPL licensed) for the UML diagrams to help you understand the design in this book. It integrates with Java projects, allowing you to model classes and their relationships directly from your code (you can learn more about it from the link: https://eclipse.dev/papyrus/). Sometimes, I also edited the generated diagrams for better readability. **You can safely assume that these diagrams help you understand the code, but neither Papyrus nor Eclipse is mandatory to follow the book.**

Conventions Used in This Book

To keep the examples organized, each demonstration in this book is placed in its own package (for example, demo1, demo2), and the client code for each demonstration is placed in the corresponding .client subpackage. The common code that is used by multiple demonstrations is placed in a separate package as well. For example, you'll find all demonstrations for the Factory pattern (discussed in Chapter 1) inside the factory package. The SimpleVehicleFactory class in this chapter was **specific** to Demonstration 2, so it is placed inside **factory.demo2** package, and the corresponding **client code** for Demonstration 2 is placed in **factory.demo2.client**. The **factory. vehicles** package, however, contains the **common code** that will be used by all demonstrations in this chapter.

Finally, all the programs, corresponding outputs, and important notes of the book follow the same font and structure. To draw your attention, in some places, I have made them bold. For example, consider the following code fragment (taken from Chapter 5, where I discussed the constructor injection technique as follows):

```java
import di.vehicles.Vehicle;

public class Driver {
    private Vehicle vehicle;
    public Driver(Vehicle vehicle) {
        this.vehicle = vehicle;
    }
    public void drive(int speed) {
        System.out.println("The driver can drive a " + vehicle.travel(speed));
    }
}
```

Final Words

You are an intelligent person. You have chosen a topic that can assist you throughout your career. As you learn and review these concepts, I suggest you write your code; only then will you master this area. There is no shortcut for this. Do you know the ancient story of Euclid and Ptolemy, ruler of Egypt? Euclid's approach to mathematics was based on logical reasoning and rigorous proofs, and Ptolemy asked Euclid if there was an easier way to learn mathematics. Euclid's reply to the ruler? **"There is no royal road to geometry."** Though you are not studying geometry, the essence of this reply applies here. You must study these concepts and code. Do not give up when you face challenges. They are the indicators that you are growing better.

Errata: I have tried my level best to ensure the accuracy of the content. However, mistakes can happen. So, I have a plan to maintain the "Errata," and if required, I can also make some updates/announcements there. So, I suggest that you visit those pages to receive any important corrections or updates.

An Appeal: You can easily understand that any good quality work takes many days and many months (even years!). Many authors like me invest most of their time in writing and heavily depend on it. You can encourage and help these authors by preventing piracy. If you come across any illegal copies of our works in any form on the internet, I would be grateful if you would provide me/the Apress team with the location address or website name. In this context, you can use the link https://www.apress.com/gp/services/rights-permission/piracy as well.

Share Your Feedback: The book is designed so that upon its completion, you will develop an adequate knowledge of creational design patterns using Java. I hope that you will value the effort. Once you finish reading this book, I request that you provide valuable feedback on the Amazon review page or any other platform you like.

CHAPTER 1

The Factory Pattern

Creating objects directly in a program may seem easy. However, as the program grows, this approach can make the code messy and hard to maintain. This chapter helps you understand the problem and explore possible solutions using factories.

Here, you'll see three demonstrations. The first one discusses **the problem of direct instantiation**, the second one discusses how the **Simple Factory** pattern can help you better organize the code, and the final one discusses how the **Factory Method** pattern can provide better support by handling object creation in a structured way to make your code cleaner and extendible.

Direct Instantiations

Consider a company that produces different types of vehicles. Can you make an application where clients can instantiate the vehicles of their choice? Of course you can. In fact, there are many ways to do this. Let's start by exploring a program that does not use a factory.

Programming Without a Factory

For simplicity, let's assume that the company currently produces only cars and motorcycles. Since both cars and motorcycles are vehicles, let's assume you start with an abstract class, named Vehicle, as follows:

© Vaskaran Sarcar 2026
V. Sarcar, *Creational Design Patterns in Java*, Apress Pocket Guides,
https://doi.org/10.1007/979-8-8688-2314-5_1

REMINDER

To avoid redundancy, the full explanation of the package structure used throughout this book is given in the **Introduction** of the book. For this chapter, remember that **each demonstration is placed in its own package**, and **its client code is kept in the corresponding .client** subpackage, while **common codes are placed in shared packages** (e.g., **factory.vehicles** in this chapter).

```java
// Vehicle.java
package factory.vehicles;

public abstract class Vehicle {
   protected String type = "vehicle";
   public void validate() {
      System.out.println("The " + this + " validation is completed.");
   }
   @Override
   public String toString() {
      return type;
   }
}
```

Author's note: Although the Vehicle class is declared as abstract, it does not define any abstract methods. It serves as a common base class to prevent direct instantiation and to allow subclasses (such as Car and Motorcycle) to specialize the type field. Here, "this" implicitly invokes the toString() method, which returns the value of the type field.

The Car and Motorcycle classes inherit from the Vehicle class. First, see the Car class:

// Car.java

```
package factory.vehicles;

public class Car extends Vehicle {
    public Car() {
        type = "car";
    }
}
```

The Motorcycle class maintains a similar structure:

// Motorcycle.java

```
package factory.vehicles;

public class Motorcycle extends Vehicle {
    public Motorcycle() {
        type = "motorcycle";
    }
}
```

Now, a client can instantiate the Car and Motorcycle classes. In the upcoming program, whenever I instantiate an object, I use the new operator. Probably, you are familiar with this approach. Before you see the client code (**FPDemo1Client.java**), let me show you the class diagram (Figure 1-1) as well.

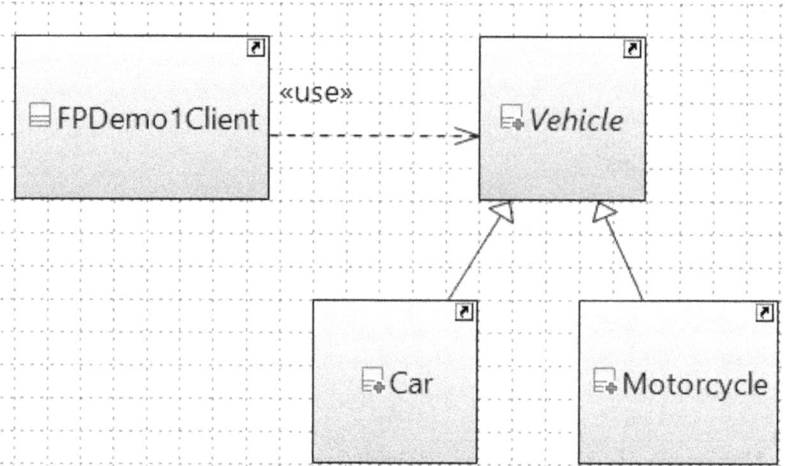

Figure 1-1. *The participants of Demonstration 1*

POINT TO NOTE

The package structure is already indicated in the code listings. The purpose of this diagram is to illustrate **class relationships**, but not the package organization. I intentionally kept this diagram simple to make it easier to read. **The same comment applies to all class diagrams in this book.**

Demonstration 1

Here is the client code:

// FPDemo1Client.java

```java
package factory.demo1.client;

import factory.vehicles.Vehicle;
import factory.vehicles.Car;
import factory.vehicles.Motorcycle;
```

```java
class FPDemo1Client {

  public static void main(String[] args) {
    System.out.println("The client does not exercise a factory.\n");
    Vehicle vehicle = createAndValidateVehicle("car");
    System.out.println("Your " + vehicle + " is now ready.");
    System.out.println("-----------");

    vehicle = createAndValidateVehicle("motorcycle");
    System.out.println("Your " + vehicle + " is now ready.");
  }

  private static Vehicle createAndValidateVehicle(String type) {
    Vehicle vehicle = null;
    if (type.equals("car")) {
      vehicle = new Car();
    } else if (type.equals("motorcycle")) {
      vehicle = new Motorcycle();
    } else {
      System.out.println("You can make either a car or a motorcycle.");
      throw new IllegalArgumentException("invalid argument: " + type);
    }
    vehicle.validate();
    return vehicle;
  }
}
```

Output

There is no surprise that when you execute this program, you'll see the
following output:

The client does not exercise a factory.

The car validation is completed.
Your car is now ready.

The motorcycle validation is completed.
Your motorcycle is now ready.

POINT TO NOTE

If you compile and run the examples in this book from the command line, ensure that you execute the **javac** and **java** commands from the parent directory of the base package (e.g., src). The directory structure must match the package declarations. However, if you use an IDE such as Eclipse, the setup and execution process are handled automatically.

Analysis

In this implementation, using the vehicle variable, you used conditional logic to pick the appropriate type of vehicle. You indeed made runtime decisions about which class to instantiate, and this is not a bad thing. However, let me ask you a few questions. **If you need a different type of vehicle (e.g., a bus), how can you proceed?** Even if you already have a Bus class, you need to change the client code by introducing a new if block, such as

```
if (type.equals("bus")) {
  vehicle = new Bus();
}
```

OK. Let me ask you another question: **If the company decides to stop the production of cars (or motorcycles), how can you proceed?** You'll delete the corresponding if block in the client code.

You can see that you may need to make changes inside the createAndValidateVehicle method very often. In other words, this client code may need to be changed at any time in the future. Let me highlight the code segment of our concern in bold:

```java
private static Vehicle createAndValidateVehicle(String type) {
    Vehicle vehicle = null;
    if (type.equals("car")) {
      vehicle = new Car();
    } else if (type.equals("motorcycle")) {
      vehicle = new Motorcycle();
    } else {
      System.out.println("You can make either a car or a motorcycle.");
      throw new IllegalArgumentException("invalid argument: " + type);
    }
    vehicle.validate();
    return vehicle;
  }
```

It means that you violate the **Open–Closed Principle (OCP)** (which basically says that a code module should be open for extension, but closed for modification) of the SOLID principles.

SOLID PRINCIPLES

The SOLID principles consist of five principles: the Single Responsibility Principle (SRP), the Open–Closed Principle (OCP), the Liskov Substitution Principle (LSP), the Interface Segregation Principle (ISP), and the Dependency Inversion Principle (DIP). The famous American engineer and author Robert C. Martin (Uncle Bob) popularized these principles. Taking the first letter of each principle, Michael Feathers introduced the SOLID acronym, so that we can remember them easily.

According to Robert C. Martin, the OCP is the most important principle among all the principles of object-oriented design. In the book *Clean Architecture* (Pearson), he acknowledged that *the Open–Closed Principle was originally coined in 1988 by Bertrand Meyer.* This principle states that **a software artifact should be open for extension but closed for modification**.

Many online sources explain the concept. I also discussed these principles in detail in my other book, *Simple and Efficient Programming with C# (Second Edition)*. However, for a quick introduction about them, you can follow the link: SOLID – Wikipedia.[1] If interested, you can learn more from the following links as well: Clean Coder – Getting a SOLID start[2] and Clean Coder Blog.[3]

It has another drawback: **in an enterprise application, different parts of the system may need to create the same type of object. As a result, the same creation code ends up being repeated in multiple places, making the situation even worse.**

Can you make a better solution? Let's analyze the upcoming demonstration.

Simple Factory Pattern

This is the time to introduce the Simple Factory pattern. Before that, let me help you understand the concept of a factory.

---

[1] https://en.wikipedia.org/wiki/SOLID

[2] https://sites.google.com/site/unclebobconsultingllc/getting-a-solid-start

[3] https://blog.cleancoder.com/uncle-bob/2020/10/18/Solid-Relevance.html

What Is a Factory?

In object-oriented programming (OOP), a factory is an object that can create other objects. A factory can be invoked in many ways, but it often uses a method that can return objects with varying prototypes. Any subroutine that can help us create these new objects can be considered a factory. Most importantly, it abstracts the process of object creation from the application's consumers. Let me give you some examples:

Real-Life Example

Suppose you visit a South Indian restaurant to enjoy a biryani dish. The waiter may ask if you'd like it extra spicy or less spicy. Depending on your preference, the chef will adjust the spices to the core material and make an appropriate dish for you. The chef acts as a factory for you in this example.

Let's consider another example: when a kid demands a toy from their parents, the kid does not know how the parents will fulfill the wish. In this case, the parent may buy the toy from a shop or even make one at home, but either way, the child simply receives the toy. From the kid's point of view, the parent acts like a factory that provides what was asked for.

Computer World Example

Suppose your application needs to connect to different databases—such as Oracle, MySQL, or Microsoft SQL Server. In such a case, you can use this pattern to create the appropriate DataSource object for each database type.

In fact, this pattern is common to software applications. **You must note that the Simple Factory pattern is not treated as a standard design pattern in GoF's famous book, but the approach is common to any application you write. The idea is simple: separate the code that changes a lot from the part of the code that does not change often.** You are assumed to follow this approach in all the applications you write.

POINT TO REMEMBER

One of the key object-oriented design principles is to identify what varies and separate it from what does not vary.

I hope you have gotten some idea about factories. Let's separate the "varying" part of the previous program (Demonstration 1) in the upcoming demonstration (Demonstration 2).

Note   In Demonstration 2, the SimpleVehicleFactory class reuses the Vehicle, Car, and Motorcycle classes of the factory.vehicle package.

Demonstration 2

Now I create another class, named SimpleVehicleFactory, that exposes the public **static** method createVehicle to create the objects. I have made this method static to allow the client to call it directly on the class without instantiating the factory. Here is the content:

```java
// SimpleVehicleFactory.java
package factory.demo2;

import factory.vehicles.Car;
import factory.vehicles.Motorcycle;
import factory.vehicles.Vehicle;

public class SimpleVehicleFactory {
  public static Vehicle createVehicle(String type) {
    Vehicle vehicle = null;
    if (type.equals("car")) {
      vehicle = new Car();
    }
```

```
  else if (type.equals("motorcycle")) {
   vehicle = new Motorcycle();
  }
  else {
   System.out.println("You can make either a car or a motorcycle.");
   throw new IllegalArgumentException("Invalid argument: "+type);
  }
  return vehicle;
 }
}
```

Congratulations! You have created a factory class!

POINTS TO NOTE

This implementation uses simple if-else conditions to select the vehicle type. A more robust version could replace these string comparisons with a **switch** statement based on an **enum** that declares all supported vehicle types.

In addition, although the factory class can still be instantiated, it is not required. **In practice, you can make the constructor private to prevent object creation since the class only provides static methods.** We'll revisit this idea of using a private constructor in the next chapter on the Singleton Pattern.

Before you see the client code (**FPDemo2Client.java**), let me show you the class diagram (Figure 1-2) as well.

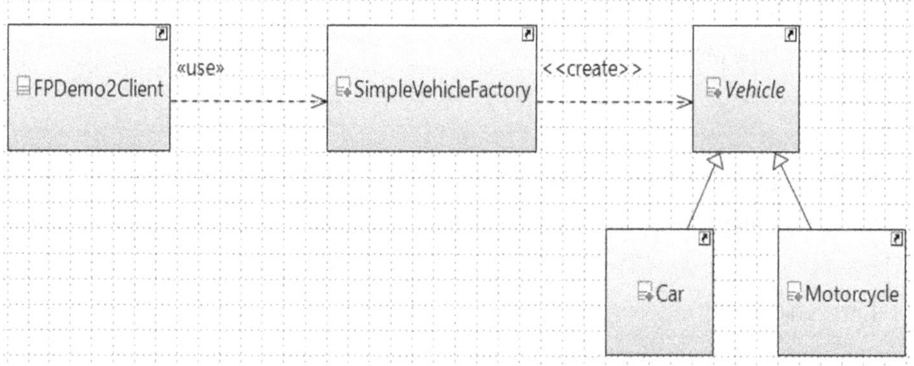

Figure 1-2. *The client uses a simple factory to create vehicles in Demonstration 2*

POINT TO NOTE

In Figure 1-2, I used the label <<create>> to show that the SimpleVehicleFactory class instantiates the vehicles. In Figure 1-3, I'll do the same to show which class instantiates which others. It's similar to the GoF book that used the OMT (Object Modeling Technique) notions. However, in the GoF book, the end arrow was filled. Since OMT didn't support this notion, they introduced that diagram to show this kind of relationship and named it the "creates" relationship.

Let me show you the client code (**FP_Demo2_Client.java**) now. This time, it is very concise (notice the createAndValidateVehicle method and the key change in bold):

// FP_Demo2_Client.java

```
package factory.demo2.client;

import factory.vehicles.Vehicle;
import factory.demo2.SimpleVehicleFactory;
```

```java
class FPDemo2Client {

  public static void main(String[] args) {
    System.out.println("Using the simple factory pattern.\n");
    Vehicle vehicle = createAndValidateVehicle("car");
    System.out.println("Your " + vehicle + " is now ready.");
    System.out.println("-----------");
    vehicle = createAndValidateVehicle("motorcycle");
    System.out.println("Your " + vehicle + " is now ready.");
  }

  private static Vehicle createAndValidateVehicle(String type) {
    Vehicle vehicle = SimpleVehicleFactory.createVehicle(type);
    vehicle.validate();
    return vehicle;
  }
}
```

Output

Once you execute the program, you'll see that, except for the first line, everything is identical to the previous output (I changed the first line to highlight that I followed the Simple Factory pattern in this demonstration). Here is the output for your ready reference:

```
Using the simple factory pattern.

The car validation is completed.
Your car is now ready.

-----------
The motorcycle validation is completed.
Your motorcycle is now ready.
```

Analysis

Now we have separated the part that creates vehicles from the part that does not vary. This is why the following lines are still present in the createAndValidateVehicle method:

```
vehicle.validate();
return vehicle;
```

As a result, if you need to change the creation process again, you'll only update it inside the SimpleVehicleFactory class (more specifically, in the createVehicle method). The client code won't need any changes, even if the requirements evolve.

Q&A Session

Q1.1 At the end, instead of using the new operator inside the client code, you used it inside the createVehicle() method. However, the use of the new operator is very common, and no one restricts us from using it inside the client code. Isn't it correct?

Each program is indeed different, and technically, there is no problem when you use the new operator to instantiate an object. However, the design of a program/software is important. If you read our discussion sequentially, it's easy to understand that I was trying to improve the program to accommodate the future changes in a better way.

For example, in the first program (Demonstration 1) of this chapter, if you need to consider a new type of vehicle, you must open the createAndValidateVehicle method, and you'll make the changes. This process violates **OCP.** In addition, I also told you that **in an enterprise application, if you end up writing the same code in multiple locations, you'll make the situation even worse.**

Q1.2 However, in Demonstration 2, I still need to open the createVehicle method to consider new vehicles. Is this correct?

In Demonstration 2, the createAndValidateVehicle was the only method that used the factory method. In other words, you have seen only one client of SimpleVehicleFactory. However, the SimpleVehicleFactory class can have many more clients who would like to use its createVehicle method.

By encapsulating the creational process in one class, you allow only one place to accommodate the upcoming changes. In fact, we already closed the createAndValidateVehicle method for modification in Demonstration 2.

Q1.3 I understand that in Demonstration 2, instead of directly creating objects, the client delegates the object's creation through the Simple Factory pattern. But what are the benefits of this design?"

Let me remind you that one of the key object-oriented design principles is to separate the parts of your code that are most likely to change from the rest. As a result, you can have the following benefits:

- **No changes in client code:** If the creation process changes in the future, you only modify the factory, not the client (such as FP_Demo2_Client.java in Demonstration 2).

- **Clearer client:** You avoid cluttering the client code with multiple if-else blocks (or switch statements).

- **Better abstraction:** How you are creating the objects is hidden from the client code. This kind of abstraction promotes security.

- **Centralized lifecycle management:** Sometimes you'd like to manage the lifecycle of created objects in a uniform way. If clients are allowed to create objects freely, you lose that control. A factory centralizes this responsibility.

Q1.4 Can you give me a built-in example of a simple factory?

The getInstance method of java.text.NumberFormat class is a typical built-in example of a simple factory. Let me open up the built-in code in Eclipse:

```java
private static NumberFormat getInstance(LocaleProviderAdapter adapter,
    Locale locale, Style formatStyle, int choice) {
    NumberFormatProvider provider = adapter.getNumberFormatProvider();
    return switch (choice) {
        case NUMBERSTYLE   -> provider.getNumberInstance(locale);
        case PERCENTSTYLE  -> provider.getPercentInstance(locale);
        case CURRENCYSTYLE -> provider.getCurrencyInstance(locale);
        case INTEGERSTYLE  -> provider.getIntegerInstance(locale);
        case COMPACTSTYLE  -> provider.getCompactNumberInstance(locale,
                                        formatStyle);
        default            -> null;
    };
}
```

You can see the following points from this code:

- The getInstance is a static method.

- The method picks the right subclass of NumberFormat based on the choice parameter.

- The creational logic is wrapped in this method. The client code stays decoupled—it knows about the NumberFormat class, but not its subclass.

This is why it is an example of a built-in simple factory pattern in Java.

SIMPLE FACTORY PROMOTES DECOUPLING

In Demonstration 2, the SimpleVehicleFactory class was used to create cars and motorcycles. This factory class allows you to decouple the object creation process from the client code (that uses those objects).

Factory Method Pattern

Now you are ready to explore the factory method pattern. The Gang of Four (GoF) mentioned the intent of the Factory Method pattern as follows:

Define an interface for creating an object, but let subclasses decide which class to instantiate. Factory Method lets a class defer instantiation to subclasses.

You can see that the GoF provides some additional suggestions for making a factory in which the subclasses handle the details. What is the benefit? Let's understand it with a case study.

POINT TO NOTE

We often use the term "program to an interface" not to describe a typical Java interface—it can be **any supertype** (abstract class, super class, or even a Java interface with default methods) that defines the construction contract.

Using Multiple Factories

Demonstration 2 works fine and meets our expectations. However, what happens if the company recognizes that making cars and motorcycles in the same place is causing chaos? Assume that to avoid the chaos, it decides to segregate the activity in different locations: in one location, it will make cars, and in another location, it will make motorcycles. **In short, the company now needs to function with multiple factories (a.k.a. branches) at different locations.**

Though we allow both factories to make products of their choice, it is safe to assume that the company will not change the final validation process to maintain its reputation and the quality of the vehicles. So, we should place the common logic in one location. **This way, both factories can reuse it, and we can avoid code duplication.**

You can see that the simple factory cannot fulfil these criteria. Let's dive into the Factory Method pattern now.

First, I'll introduce a new inheritance hierarchy where you'll see three classes: VehicleFactory, CarFactory, and MotorcycleFactory. The first one is an abstract class and contains the common code. The other classes inherit from this class and make vehicles based on their preferences. Let us see the abstract class (it contains the factory method) with the important segment in bold:

Author's note: The factories are used to make products. In a sense, they are creators of the vehicles in our examples. So, while organizing the factories in Demonstration 3, I placed them in the factory.demo3.creator package.

// VehicleFactory.java

```
package factory.demo3.creator;

import factory.vehicles.Vehicle;

public abstract class VehicleFactory
{
    public Vehicle createAndValidateVehicle()
    {
        Vehicle vehicle= createVehicle();
```

```java
    vehicle.validate();
    return vehicle;
  }

  // This is the "factory method". Notice that I defer the
  // instantiation process to the subclasses.
  protected abstract Vehicle createVehicle();
}
```

You can see the createVehicle method is abstract and **non-static** now (I used the protected modifier to restrict the access of this member to this class and its subclasses only). So, a subclass of VehicleFactory needs to implement this method (otherwise, it will be abstract again). Once you get the appropriate vehicle, the createAndValidateVehicle method will invoke the validate method to validate the product (this is the common code for the vehicles).

I already told you that the VehicleFactory class has two subclasses: CarFactory and MotorcycleFactory. Let's see the CarFactory class:

```java
// CarFactory.java
package factory.demo3.creator;

import factory.vehicles.Car;
import factory.vehicles.Vehicle;

public class CarFactory extends VehicleFactory {
  @Override
  protected Vehicle createVehicle() {
    return new Car();
  }
}
```

Now see the MotorcycleFactory class that also inherits from the VehicleFactory class:

// MotorcycleFactory.java

```java
package factory.demo3.creator;

package factory.demo3.creator;

import factory.vehicles.Motorcycle;
import factory.vehicles.Vehicle;

public class MotorcycleFactory extends VehicleFactory {
  @Override
  protected Vehicle createVehicle() {
    return new Motorcycle();
  }
}
```

Congratulations once again! You have implemented the factory pattern following the GoF way, where the concrete factories create cars and motorcycles.

To make things easy for you, before I present the client code (**FPDemo3Client.java**), let me show you the key participants in the following class diagram (see Figure 1-3).

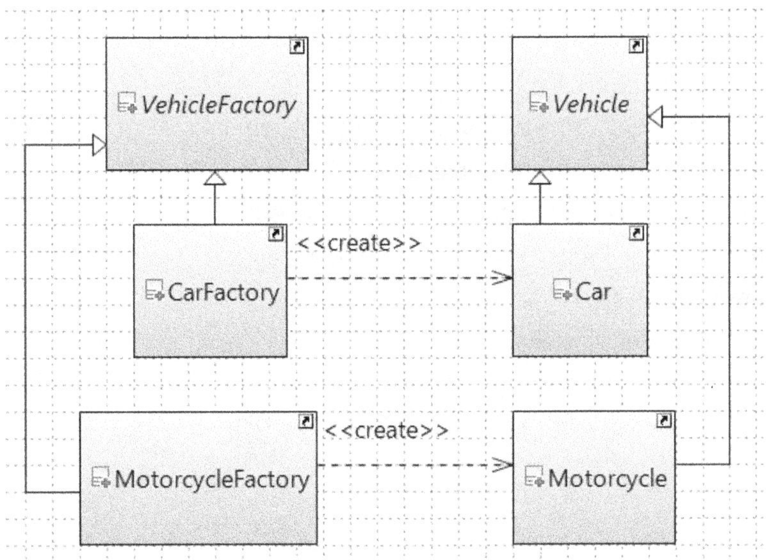

Figure 1-3. *The key participants in Demonstration 3. The client that uses the VehicleFactory hierarchy is omitted here to keep the diagram simple*

Demonstration 3

Let's see the client code (**FPDemo3Client.java**). I want you to note that in the client code, each concrete factory (such as CarFactory or MotorcycleFactory) must first be instantiated before invoking the createAndValidateVehicle() method now.

// FPDemo3Client.java

```
package factory.demo3.client;

import factory.demo3.creator.VehicleFactory;
import factory.demo3.creator.CarFactory;
import factory.demo3.creator.MotorcycleFactory;
import factory.vehicles.Vehicle;
```

```java
class FPDemo3Client {

    public static void main(String[] args) {
        System.out.println("Using the Factory Method pattern.\n");
        VehicleFactory factory= new CarFactory();
        Vehicle vehicle = factory.createAndValidateVehicle();
        System.out.println("Your " + vehicle + " is now ready.");
        System.out.println("-----------");
        factory = new MotorcycleFactory();
        vehicle = factory.createAndValidateVehicle();
        System.out.println("Your " + vehicle + " is now ready.");
    }
}
```

Output

Once you execute the program, you'll see the following output (once again, except for the first line, the remaining output is identical):

```
Using the Factory Method pattern.

The car validation is completed.
Your car is now ready.
-----------
The motorcycle validation is completed.
Your motorcycle is now ready.
```

Q&A Session

Q1.5 What are the advantages of using a factory like this?

Here are some key advantages:

- **Easier maintenance:** You are separating the code that varies from the code that does not vary (in other words, the advantages of using the Simple Factory pattern are still present). This helps you to maintain the code easily.

- **OCP compliance:** According to the *Open–Closed Principle (OCP)*, software entities should be open for extension but closed for modification. Here, if you'd like to add a new product, say Bus, you can simply create a BusFactory—no changes are required to the existing architecture.

- **Encapsulation of creation logic:** The client does not need to know *how* a product object is instantiated—the factory encapsulates this logic and provides a clean interface for object creation.

Author's note: However, in this case, the client must first create (or obtain) an appropriate factory instance before using it. In some designs, factories themselves can be implemented as Singletons (discussed in Chapter 2)to ensure only one factory instance is created and shared.

Q1.6 Should we always mark the creator class (the class containing the factory method) as abstract, so that subclasses can provide the concrete implementation?

No, the creator class does not always have to be abstract. Instead, it can be a concrete class that may provide a default implementation for the factory method. The classical GoF book confirms the following variations of this pattern:

- The Creator is an abstract class, and it does not provide the factory method implementation (the implementation you saw in Demonstration 3).

- The Creator is a concrete class and provides a default implementation for the factory method.

- The Creator is an abstract class, but it provides a concrete (default) implementation of the factory method. Subclasses may override this method if needed. This variation is less common.

Q1.7 I see that the creators and their creations are forming separate class hierarchies in Demonstration 3. Is this correct?

You are an excellent reader. Your observation is correct.

Q1.8 Can you give me a built-in example of the factory method?

You can consider the iterator method of java.util.AbstractCollection is a built-in example of the factory method. Let's retrieve its definition in the Eclipse IDE:

```java
public abstract class AbstractCollection<E> implements Collection<E> {

  // Previous code skipped
   /**
     * Returns an iterator over the elements contained in this collection.
     *
     * @return an iterator over the elements contained in this collection
     */
    public abstract Iterator<E> iterator();

  // Remaining code skipped
}
```

This means that **subclasses must provide their own concrete implementation** of the iterator() method. Let's trace it with ArrayList. The ArrayList class extends AbstractList, which already provides a **default implementation** of iterator(). However, ArrayList chooses to **override** it with its own specialized implementation:

```java
public class ArrayList<E> extends AbstractList<E>
    implements List<E>, RandomAccess, Cloneable, java.io.Serializable
{

// Previous code skipped
  /**
    * Returns an iterator over the elements in this list in proper sequence.
    *
    * <p>The returned iterator is <a href="#fail-fast"><i>fail-fast</i></a>.
    *
    * @return an iterator over the elements in this list in proper sequence
    */
  public Iterator<E> iterator() {
     return new Itr();
  }

 // Remaining code is skipped
}
```

Q1.9 Can you discuss the difference between the Simple Factory and Factory Method patterns?

The Simple Factory pattern is easy to use. It centralizes object creation in one place. However, any change in product types (such as adding or removing products) forces us to modify the factory class, thereby violating the **Open–Closed Principle (OCP)**.

For example, in Demonstration 2, if you need to introduce a new vehicle, you must update the conditional logic inside the SimpleVehicleFactory class. This means that to accommodate new requirements, you are compelled to change the factory class itself. In this sense, the Simple Factory can be seen as a **"one-time deal"**—flexible only until the first new requirement arises.

Now compare this with the **Factory Method** implementation in **Demonstration 3**. Here, the createAndValidateVehicle() method calls the abstract createVehicle() method. The client decides **what** type of product to create by choosing a specific factory (e.g., CarFactory or MotorcycleFactory), but it does not know **how** the object is actually created. The instantiation details remain hidden within the concrete factory subclass, which encapsulates the creation logic.

This makes the Factory Method more **flexible and extensible**, since classes don't need to anticipate the possible product(s) in advance. If you want to add a new type of vehicle—say, a Bicycle—you can simply create a new BicycleFactory that produces Bicycle instances. You don't need to modify the existing architecture, so your design remains **OCP-compliant**. The trade-off is that you need to manage **more factory classes** compared to the Simple Factory approach, which can lead to a "class explosion" as the number of product types increases.

In summary, the Factory Method pattern provides a framework where different subclasses can produce different products, while the Simple Factory cannot vary its products in a similar way.

To visualize the difference, Figures 1-4 and 1-5 illustrate how the client interacts with the factories.

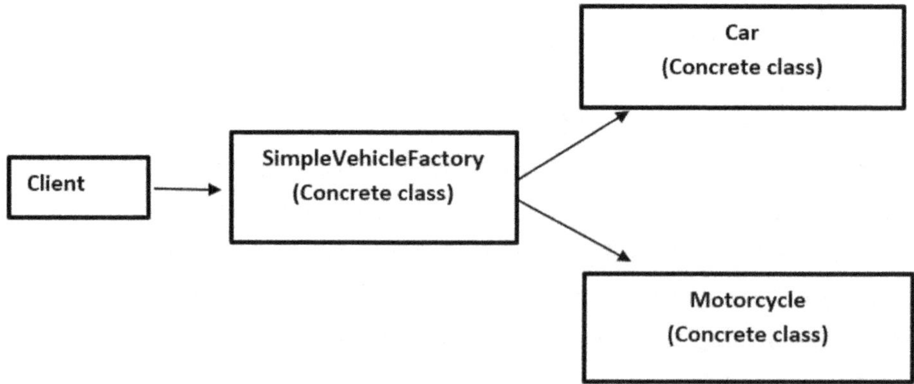

Figure 1-4. *The workflow in Demonstration 2 that uses the Simple Factory pattern)*

The following figure (Figure 1-5) shows how the client used the Factory Method pattern and received factory-specific products.

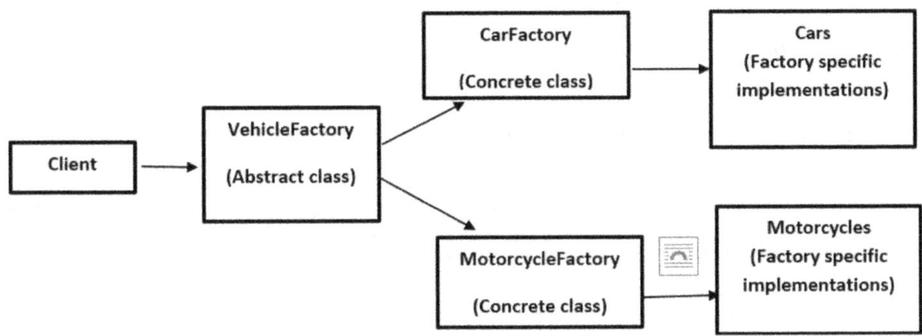

Figure 1-5. *The workflow in Demonstration 3 that uses the Factory Method pattern*

Q1.10 If I follow Demonstration 3 whenever I'd like to add a new type of vehicle—say, a SportsCar—I need to consider a new concrete factory class, say SportsCarFactory. It makes me uncomfortable. The Car class could accommodate this variation. Is this correct?

Good observation. If adding a new subtype always forces you to add a new factory, it can indeed feel like overhead. One way to reduce this is to use a **parameterized factory method**. With this approach, you can ask a factory, *"Give me a regular car"* or *"Give me a sports car"* by simply passing a parameter—rather than writing separate factory classes for each variation.

But **here's the trade-off: while parameterization gives you more flexibility, you do compromise a bit on OCP compliance**. For example, in *Appendix A: Exploring Pattern Enhancements*, you'll see me extending Demonstration 3. There, we assume that the CarFactory can produce different types of cars (e.g., regular cars and sports cars), and the MotorcycleFactory can produce different types of motorcycles (e.g., regular motorcycles and sports motorcycles).

In that implementation, the abstract factory class (VehicleFactory) stays closed for modification, but the concrete factories (like CarFactory or MotorcycleFactory) must change to support new variations. Later, I'll also show an alternative implementation that adheres more strictly to OCP.

At the end of the day, our goal is not to blindly follow a pattern or principle, but to make **high-quality, maintainable software**.

LOOKING AHEAD

Sometimes, we may want to create objects in ways that the basic patterns don't fully cover—for example, handling dynamic parameters or variations. Some of these enhanced techniques, along with code refactoring, are discussed in **Appendix A: Exploring Pattern Enhancements. There you'll see more implementations covering parameterized factory and registry-based factory patterns**.

Summary

This chapter showed you three demonstrations covering **the problem of direct instantiation**, the **Simple Factory** pattern, and the **Factory Method** pattern. Along the way, you learned how factories make your code more organized, flexible, and easier to extend. In addition, you saw the key differences between Simple Factory and Factory Method. With these foundations in place, you're ready to move on to the next chapter.

CHAPTER 2

Singleton Pattern

The Singleton pattern can be implemented in many ways, each with its own pros and cons. This chapter explores four different implementations and their advantages, along with the trade-offs.

Concept

The Gang of Four (GoF) defined the intent of the Singleton pattern as follows:

> *Ensure a class only has one instance, and provide a global point of access to it.*

Let's assume you have a class named Sample and you need to create an object from it. Normally, what would you do? You guessed it right; you can simply use the following line of code:

```
Sample sample = new Sample();
```

But let's see it closely. Each time you use the new keyword, a fresh object is created. Right? But in a real-world scenario, managing a large number of objects is a big concern (particularly when constructor calls are costly), and you'd like to restrict this. In a situation like this, the Singleton pattern comes into the picture. It restricts the use of the new operator and ensures that you do not have more than one instance of the class.

© Vaskaran Sarcar 2026
V. Sarcar, *Creational Design Patterns in Java*, Apress Pocket Guides,
https://doi.org/10.1007/979-8-8688-2314-5_2

Since Java's garbage collector manages memory efficiently, you may still ask **why we should care about object creation at all**. In large systems, object creation can easily reach millions of instances, putting pressure on the garbage collector and degrading performance. Moreover, since RAM is not infinite, excessive object creation can quickly exhaust available memory.

How does the Singleton pattern overcome this problem? It suggests that a particular class should have only one instance. If an instance is unavailable, you can create one; otherwise, you should use the existing one to serve your needs.

Real-Life Example

Let's assume you have a sports team and the team is participating in a tournament. Your team needs to play against multiple opponents throughout the tournament. At the beginning of each of these matches, as per the game's rules, the captains of the two sides must go for a coin toss. So, if your team does not have a captain, you need to elect someone as a captain first. Before each game and each coin toss, your team does not repeat the process of electing a captain if the team has already nominated a captain for this tournament. In this example, selecting a captain is like creating a new object, while retaining the same captain for all matches represents reusing the existing instance.

Computer World Example

In some software systems, you may decide to maintain only one file system so that you can use it for the centralized management of resources. This approach can help you implement caching mechanisms effectively. This pattern can also be used to maintain a thread pool in a multithreading environment.

Author's note: You may also note that the built-in java.lang.Runtime class follows this pattern (Q2.7 discusses this in detail).

The First Implementation

The Singleton pattern can be implemented in several ways, each with its own pros and cons. Let us explore some of them in this chapter.

Using the Synchronized Method

In the first demonstration, I use a synchronized method to illustrate the Singleton pattern. Here, you'll see a class called Captain. To prevent external instantiation, I use a private constructor. As a result, inside the client code, you cannot write something like the following:

```
Captain captain = new Captain(); // Error
```

I have also made the Captain class final. So, you cannot write something like the following as well:

```
public class Derived extends Captain { } // Error
```

Note   Since I already had the private constructor, I could avoid using the final keyword in this demonstration. Then why did I make the class final? Because a final class cannot be extended. It can be beneficial if you make some specific modifications. You'll see a discussion on this in Q2.2.

You'll see that the getCaptainInstance() method in the Captain class provides controlled access to its single instance. Clients can use this method to obtain the shared Captain object. This method is declared as static and synchronized, which means it can be called without creating an object, and multiple threads cannot execute it simultaneously. Together, these modifiers ensure controlled, thread-safe access to the single instance during creation. Let's see the Captain class now:

// Captain.java

```java
package singleton.demo1;
public final class Captain {
   private static Captain CAP_INSTANCE;
   // The private constructor prevents the use of "new" outside of this class
   private Captain() {
    System.out.println("A new captain is elected.");
   }
   public static synchronized Captain getCaptainInstance() {
   // Lazy initialization
   if (CAP_INSTANCE == null) {
    CAP_INSTANCE = new Captain();
   } else {
     System.out.println("The existing captain will go for the coin toss.");
   }
   return CAP_INSTANCE;
   }
}
```

Author's note: You might wonder why CAP_INSTANCE is not declared as final. Since this demonstration uses lazy initialization, the instance is created only when it is first requested. Declaring it as final would require immediate assignment, which contradicts the lazy initialization strategy.

To simplify things, before you see the client code (SPDemo1Client.java), let's visualize the class diagram of this Captain class (see Figure 2-1) as well.

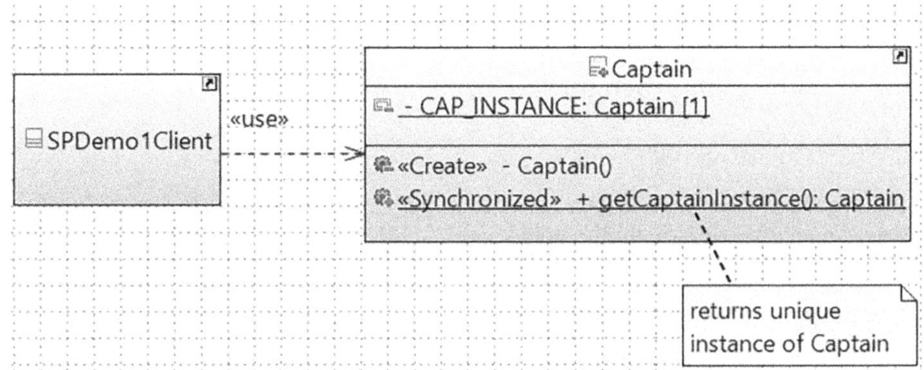

Figure 2-1. *The application can create only one Captain instance that can be accessed via getCaptainInstance()*

Demonstration 1

Here is a sample code that uses the Captain class as follows:

// SPDemo1Client.java

```java
package singleton.demo1.client;

import singleton.demo1.Captain;

class SPDemo1Client {
  public static void main(String[] args) {
    System.out.println("Selecting a captain for your team.");
     createOrUseCaptain();
  }
    private static void createOrUseCaptain() {
      Captain captain1 = Captain.getCaptainInstance();
      Captain captain2 = Captain.getCaptainInstance();
  }
}
```

Output

Upon executing this program, you'll get the following output:

```
Selecting a captain for your team.
A new captain is elected.
The existing captain will go for the coin toss.
```

Analysis

You can see that "A new captain is elected." has appeared only once in this output. **Congratulations! You have learned to model a singleton pattern.**

Author's note: You can also verify that only one captain is created by comparing both references (captain1 == captain2), as shown in bold in the following code segment:

```
private static void createOrUseCaptain() {
   Captain captain1 = Captain.getCaptainInstance();
   //System.out.println("Trying to involve another captain.");
   Captain captain2 = Captain.getCaptainInstance();
   // Verifies that both references point to the same instance
   if (captain1 == captain2) {
     System.out.println("Only one captain is created in this application.");
   }
}
// There is no other change in the remaining program
```

If you execute this updated program, you'll now see an additional line in the output: "**Only one captain is created in this application.**"

However, I want you to be aware of a potential drawback: since the getCaptainInstance method is synchronized, every call to this method must acquire the method-level lock (even after the first object has been created). This adds a small amount of overhead and can impact performance in applications where the method is called frequently.

In practice, the performance penalty is negligible for most use cases, but in high-concurrency systems, developers may look for alternative solutions such as **eager initialization** (discussed in Demonstration 2) or **Bill Pugh's Singleton implementation** (discussed in Demonstration 3).

Author's note: Starting with Java 21 and further in JDK 24 (see JEP 491[1]), several scalability enhancements—including those related to synchronization—have been introduced. Although I used traditional Java threads (also known as **platform threads** in newer Java releases) in some examples in this book, interested readers can refer to ongoing improvements, such as **virtual threads**. Some developers have written explicit articles on this topic. Here is a sample for your easy reference: JDK 24's Major Improvement: Virtual Threads Without Pinning.

Q&A Session

Q2.1 On my computer, I always see this output. So, it appears to me that I do not need to make the getCaptainInstance() method synchronized. Am I right?

By making the getCaptainInstance() method synchronized, you guard your application in a multithreaded environment. In a multithreaded environment, if you remove the synchronized keyword from the getCaptainInstance() method, multiple threads may create separate captains. To illustrate, let's do the following things:

- As proposed, remove the synchronized keyword from the getCaptainInstance() method definition. I have kept this non-synchronized version of Captain.java in the singleton. demo1.qa2q1 package.

Author's note: I used **qa2q1** to indicate **Question/Answer 2.1**. Similarly, **qa2q2** will be used for **Question/Answer 2.2**.

---

[1] https://openjdk.org/jeps/491

- Replace the createOrUseCaptain() method (that was used in Demonstration 1), with a new method, called verifyMultithreadedEnvironment(), in the following client code (SPDemo1Q2_1ExecutorClient.java) as follows (notice the key changes in bold):

POINT TO NOTE

You can see that the synchronized version of Captain that was used in Demonstration 1 earlier is commented out now. The following client code uses the non-synchronized version of Captain that is stored in the singleton.demo1. qa2q1 package.

```java
package singleton.demo1.client;

// import singleton.demo1.Captain; // Using the synchronized Captain
import singleton.demo1.qa2q1.Captain; // Using the non-synchronized Captain

import java.util.concurrent.ExecutorService;
import java.util.concurrent.Executors;
import java.util.concurrent.TimeUnit;

class SPDemo1Q2_1ExecutorClient {
  public static void main(String[] args) {
    System.out.println("Selecting a captain for your team.");
    verifyMultithreadedEnvironment();
  }

  private static void verifyMultithreadedEnvironment() {
    // Testing in a multithreaded environment
    ExecutorService executor = Executors.newFixedThreadPool(2);
    Runnable task = () -> {
```

```
    Captain captain = Captain.getCaptainInstance();
};
executor.submit(task);
executor.submit(task);
executor.shutdown();
try {
  executor.awaitTermination(5, TimeUnit.SECONDS);
} catch (InterruptedException e) {
  e.printStackTrace();
}
  System.out.println("Both tasks have finished execution.");
  }
}
```

POINTS TO NOTE

The ExecutorService interface provides a higher-level replacement for directly
managing threads. To explore its capabilities further, you can refer to the
official documentation: https://docs.oracle.com/en/java/javase/25/docs/api/
java.base/java/util/concurrent/ExecutorService.html. In addition, because the
awaitTermination() method throws an InterruptedException, you must wrap
it in a try-catch block to handle potential interruptions while waiting for task
completion.

**Upon executing this code, I often see that "A new captain is elected."
appears multiple times in the output.** Here is such a sample from my
computer:

```
Selecting a captain for your team.
A new captain is elected.
A new captain is elected.
Both tasks have finished execution.
```

Now make the getCaptainInstance method synchronized and execute the client code again. **Alternatively, you can simply comment out the non-synchronized version of the Captain class and uncomment the synchronized version of it as follows:**

```
package singleton.demo1.client;

 import singleton.demo1.Captain; // The synchronized Captain
//import singleton.demo1.qa2q1.Captain; // The non-synchronized Captain

// There is no change in the remaining code
```

Upon executing the program, this time, you'll see the following output:

Selecting a captain for your team.
A new captain is elected.
The existing captain will go for the coin toss.
Both tasks have finished execution.

You can see that the captain is selected only once. These sample outputs demonstrate **the effectiveness of the synchronized method** in a multithreaded application.

Author's note: If you are not familiar with ExecutorService, you can perform a similar test by using two Thread objects directly. For completeness, I have included that version in the file SPDemo1Q2_1ThreadClient.java. For your immediate reference, let me show you the content as well:

```
package singleton.demo1.client;

// import singleton.demo1.Captain; // The synchronized Captain
import singleton.demo1.qa2q1.Captain; // The non-synchronized Captain
```

```
class ExecuteTask implements Runnable {
  @Override
  public void run() {
    Captain captain = Captain.getCaptainInstance();
  }
}
class SPDemo1Q2_1ThreadClient {
  public static void main(String[] args) {
    System.out.println("Selecting a captain for your team.");
    verifyMultithreadedEnvironmentAgain();
  }
  private static void verifyMultithreadedEnvironmentAgain() {
    Thread task1 = new Thread(new ExecuteTask());
    Thread task2 = new Thread(new ExecuteTask());
    task1.start();
    task2.start();
  }
}
```

As before, when executing this code, I often see the following output:

```
Selecting a captain for your team.
A new captain is elected.
A new captain is elected.
```

Again, you can see that the captain is elected twice. However, when verifying such scenarios, the ExecutorService approach is generally preferred for its cleaner and more controlled execution.

POINT TO REMEMBER

You must remember that, depending on how your system schedules threads, you may occasionally see that only one captain is elected even after removing the synchronized keyword. This happens because thread scheduling is nondeterministic—sometimes one thread completes creating the captain before the second thread starts. However, the underlying race condition still exists, and in real-world multithreaded applications, this can lead to unpredictable results.

Q2.2 Since the Captain class already includes the private constructor, I do not see the need to use the final keyword at the class declaration. Is this correct?

Let us exercise a program, where the Captain class is **not** declared as final, and you add a nested non-static class (also known as inner class), named CaptainDerived, inside the Captain class as follows (notice the key changes in bold):

Note   You can see this version of the Captain class in the singleton. demo1.qa2q2 package.

---

package singleton.demo1.qa2q2;

```java
public class Captain {
    private static Captain CAP_INSTANCE;
    // The private constructor prevents the use of "new" outside of this class
    private Captain() {
        System.out.println(" A new captain is elected.");
    }
```

```java
public static synchronized Captain getCaptainInstance() {
 // Lazy initialization
 if (CAP_INSTANCE == null) {
  CAP_INSTANCE = new Captain();
 } else{
 System.out.println(" The existing captain will go for the coin toss.");
 }
  return CAP_INSTANCE;
 }
 // The following code block is added to discuss Q2.1
 public class CaptainDerived extends Captain
 {
 // Some other code, if any
 }
}
```

Now, let the following client exercise the following code:

```java
// SPDemo1Q2_2Client.java

package singleton.demo1.client;

import singleton.demo1.qa2q2.Captain;

class SPDemo1Q2_2Client {
  public static void main(String[] args) {
    System.out.println("Selecting a captain for your team.");
    Captain captain = Captain.getCaptainInstance();
    Captain.CaptainDerived derived1 = captain.new CaptainDerived();
    Captain.CaptainDerived derived2 = captain.new CaptainDerived();
  }
}
```

Once you execute the program, you'll see the following output:

Selecting a captain for your team.
 A new captain is elected.
 A new captain is elected.
 A new captain is elected.

This output confirms that each time you instantiate the Captain. CaptainDerived class, a new captain is elected. This happens because an inner class can access all private members of its outer class, including private constructors. Therefore, by marking the Captain class as final, you safeguard against subclass-based violations that could bypass the Singleton constraint.

Q2.3 I understand that by restricting object creations in an application, we can reduce the GC's load. However, I'd like to know whether there are any more concerns.

You can keep the following points in mind as well:

- Object creations in the real world can be costly if you work with resource-intensive objects.

- In some cases, the creation of objects is time-consuming, and it may not be a one-step process (you will learn more about this in the **Builder** pattern (discussed in Chapter 3)

- In many applications, we need a single coordinated access to a shared resource—for example, a configuration manager, a logging service, or a printer spooler. Without Singleton, multiple instances could lead to inconsistent states or resource conflicts.

In short, since this pattern offers centralized control and avoids redundant object creation, you'll value this pattern in specific scenarios.

Alternative Implementations

While designing the Singleton pattern, you can follow different approaches. You have already seen an example. Let me present a few more for you.

Eager Initialization

In this second approach, I'll discuss eager initialization, in which an object of the singleton class is always instantiated at the beginning. Let's see it in the following demonstration.

Demonstration 2

Here is the new look of the Captain class:

POINT TO NOTE

The CAP_INSTANCE variable is now declared static final because the instance is created eagerly at class-loading time and is never reassigned. Marking it as final ensures that the reference to the singleton instance cannot be modified after initialization.

```
package singleton.demo2;

public final class Captain {
    private static final Captain CAP_INSTANCE = new Captain();
    // The private constructor prevents the use of "new" outside of this class
    private Captain() {
        System.out.println(" A new captain is elected.");
    }
```

```java
    public static  Captain getCaptainInstance() {
        System.out.println(" The existing captain will go for the coin toss.");
        return CAP_INSTANCE;
    }
}
```

Output

You can use this Captain class with the same client code that you saw in SPDemo1Client.java. For example, similar to Demonstration 1, if you use createOrUseCaptain() method in the client code as follows:

```java
package singleton.demo2;

class SPDemo2Client {
    public static void main(String[] args) {
        System.out.println("Selecting a captain for your team.");
        createOrUseCaptain();
    }
    // There is no change in the createOrUseCaptain() method
    // that you saw in Demonstration 1
}
```

you'll see the following output:

```
Selecting a captain for your team.
A new captain is elected.
The existing captain will go for the coin toss.
The existing captain will go for the coin toss.
```

You can see the captain was already elected before you invoked the getCaptainInstance method.

POINT TO NOTE

In all these different approaches, the client code is essentially the same. For brevity, I did not show it repeatedly in these discussions. However, I have placed them separately in the corresponding packages. For example, SPDemo1Client.java is used as a client in Demonstration 1 and kept in singleton.demo1.client package. Similarly, SPDemo2Client.java is used as the client in Demonstration 2 and kept in singleton.demo2.client package, and so on. In addition, to verify the application in a multithreaded environment, you can use the verifyMultithreadedEnvironment method that you saw in Q2.1.

Analysis

This approach is straightforward, inherently thread-safe, and cleaner. However, the application will take a little bit more time to start (compared to the previous design), because everything needs to be loaded first.

To examine this, let us add a dummy method (shown in bold) in the singleton class.

```java
package singleton.demo2;

final class Captain {
  private static final Captain CAP_INSTANCE = new Captain();
    // The private constructor prevents the use of "new" outside of this class
    private Captain() {
      System.out.println("A new captain is elected.");
    }
    public static  Captain getCaptainInstance() {
      System.out.println("The existing captain will go for the coin toss.");
      return CAP_INSTANCE;
    }
    // Used only for an analysis of this model
```

```java
    public static void dummyMethod(){
      System.out.println("It is a dummy method.");
  }
}
```

Let us exercise the following code now:

```java
package singleton.demo2;

class SPDemo2Client {
  public static void main(String[] args) {
    Captain.dummyMethod();
    // The previous code is omitted
  }
}
```

This time, you'll see the following output:

A new captain is elected.
It is a dummy method.

You can see that "A new captain is elected" has appeared in this output, though you may have no intention to deal with that. Now you can see that **although eager initialization simplifies synchronization concerns, it may cause unnecessary resource loading at startup—even if the instance is never actually used.**

Q&A Session

Q2.4 What do you mean by the term "lazy initialization?

It's a technique that you use to delay the object creation process. The basic idea is: you should create the object only when it is truly required. This approach is useful when object creation is a costly operation for you.

Q2.5 Now I have a concern about the example of *Eager Initialization.* Following the definition, it appears to me that it is also not exactly "eager." I understand that this class will be loaded by the JVM only when it is referenced by some code during the execution of the application. In that sense, isn't this also a form of lazy initialization?

I appreciate your observation. There is indeed some debate around this topic. In short, this approach is eager relative to the previous one. As you saw, when you called only the dummyMethod(), the singleton instance was still created even though you didn't need it. **In that context, it behaves eagerly.**

However, the instantiation will not occur until the class is loaded and initialized by the JVM—and that happens only when the class is first referenced. So, in a broader sense, it is still "lazy" at the class-loading level.

So, the degree of eagerness (or laziness) depends on where you draw the boundary.

- It is "Eager" when compared to the lazy initialization approach, where creation is delayed until the getCaptainInstance method runs.

- It is "Lazy" relative to the JVM's actual class-loading process, as no resources are consumed until the class is first used.

Q2.6 You said that the built-in java.lang.Runtime class follows this pattern. Can you explain the details?

Let's retrieve the details of the java.lang.Runtime class from the Eclipse IDE:

```java
public class Runtime {
    private static final Runtime currentRuntime = new Runtime();

    private static Version version;
```

```
// The documentation comments are skipped here
public static Runtime getRuntime() {
   return currentRuntime;
}

/** Don't let anyone else instantiate this class */
private Runtime() {}
```

// Remaining code is skipped

Now, if you compare this code with the Captain class used in Demonstration 2, you'll easily find the similarities, and you can eventually conclude that it follows the Singleton pattern and **uses eager initialization**.

Bill Pugh's Singleton

Let me now show you the third approach, known as Bill Pugh's Singleton. In the earlier days (prior to Java 5), there were many issues when dealing with singleton classes. To overcome those situations, Bill Pugh proposed a solution using a static nested helper class. Using his idea, let me refactor the Captain class now.

Author's note: This approach is also known as the **lazy initialization holder idiom, lazy loaded singleton,** or **initialization-on-demand holder idiom.**

Demonstration 3

Here is the implementation with the key changes in bold:

POINT TO NOTE

I have introduced the firstCall variable to make the output consistent with previous demonstrations only. So, it is safe to assume that in a production environment, this variable and its conditional logic would typically be omitted.

```java
package singleton.demo3;

public final class Captain {
  private Captain() {
    System.out.println("A new captain is elected.");
  }
  // To track the first-time creation
  private static boolean firstCall = true;
  // The static nested helper class
  private static class CaptainHolder {
    // This nested class is referenced after the getCaptainInstance() method is called.
    private static final Captain CAP_INSTANCE = new Captain();
  }
  public static Captain getCaptainInstance() {
  if (firstCall) {
    firstCall = false; // Set flag after first access
  } else {
    System.out.println("The existing captain will go for the coin toss.");
  }
  return CaptainHolder.CAP_INSTANCE;
  }
}
```

Output

You can use this Captain class with the same client code that you saw in SPDemo1Client.java. For example, similar to Demonstration 1, if you use createOrUseCaptain() method in the client code, you'll see the following output:

Selecting a captain for your team.
A new captain is elected.
The existing captain will go for the coin toss.

Analysis

Once again, I have made the Captain class final. This prevents other classes from extending it, which could otherwise break the Singleton property. It is now combined with the static nested class to ensure a **lazy, thread-safe, and robust Singleton implementation**.

Why? Notice that the CaptainHolder class comes into consideration only when someone invokes the getCaptainInstance method. And this approach will not create any unwanted output if you call any dummyMethod inside the client code (we analyzed this case in Demonstration 2).

Enum-Based Singleton

Let me now show you the **fourth approach**, known as the **Enum-based Singleton**. Joshua Bloch, a renowned software engineer and author of *Effective Java*, showed that we can use an enum type to implement the Singleton pattern. Even though conventional singleton implementations (synchronized method, eager initialization, and Bill Pugh's approach) are widely used, enum-based singletons are very **simple and inherently thread-safe.** Let's see how it works.

Demonstration 4

In this example, we do not create a separate class or instance explicitly because the enum type itself acts as the Singleton class. The Java language specification guarantees that each enum constant is instantiated only once, and no additional instances can be created. This is why it is a natural fit for implementing the Singleton pattern. Here is a sample implementation for you:

POINT TO NOTE

I have used the private constructor to make the line "A new captain is elected." appear in the output. Why? It helps you compare this approach with the previous approaches. So, it is safe to assume that in a production environment, this constructor can be omitted.

```
package singleton.demo4;

public enum Captain {
   INSTANCE;
   private Captain() {
      System.out.println("A new captain is elected.);
   }
   public static Captain getCaptainInstance() {
      System.out.println("The existing captain will go for the coin toss.");
      return INSTANCE;
   }
}
```

Author's note: In the previous demonstrations, I used the CAP_INSTANCE variable. However, in this demonstration, I used INSTANCE following the Java naming convention for enum constants.

Output

You can use this Captain class with the same client code that you used earlier. For example, similar to Demonstration 1, if you use the createOrUseCaptain() method in the client code, you'll see the following output:

Selecting a captain for your team.
A new captain is elected.
The existing captain will go for the coin toss.
The existing captain will go for the coin toss.

You can see the captain was already elected before you invoked the getCaptainInstance method (similar to Demonstration 2).

Analysis

Since enum-based Singleton is inherently **thread-safe**, there is no synchronized keyword. Moreover, an enum type cannot be subclassed (it behaves as if it were final). These properties ensure controlled instantiation and make the enum approach naturally suited for Singleton implementation.

However, there are potential drawbacks as well: you can see that this approach does not support lazy initialization. In addition, because an enum cannot extend another class, it does **not support inheritance-based polymorphism**.

Therefore, while this approach is ideal for simple singleton use cases (such as configuration managers or loggers), it may not suit scenarios where the singleton class must participate in a class hierarchy or implement extensive business logic.

Q&A Session

Q2.7 What Class type within the Enum is expected to be created?

When you define an enum in Java, the Java compiler automatically generates a final class that extends java.lang.Enum. For example, after decompiling the code (javap -c Captain) on my computer, I got the following declaration:

```
public final class singleton.demo4.Captain extends
java.lang.Enum<singleton.demo4.Captain> {
   public static final singleton.demo4.Captain INSTANCE;
   // The remaining code is skipped
```

This confirms that "enum Captain" is converted into the "final class Captain".

Q2.8 It'd help if you throw some light on how INSTANCE was initialized.

To understand this, you need to look a bit deeper into the machine-level (bytecode) instructions. To illustrate, in my decompiled version, I could see the following static block:

```
static {};
  Code:
      0: new         #1   // class singleton/demo4/Captain
      3: dup
      4: ldc         #42  // String INSTANCE
      6: iconst_0
      7: invokespecial #43   // Method "<init>":(Ljava/lang/String;I)V
     10: putstatic    #3    // Field INSTANCE:Lsingleton/demo4/Captain;
     13: invokestatic  #44   // Method $values:()[Lsingleton/demo4/Captain;
     16: putstatic    #7    // Field $VALUES:[Lsingleton/demo4/Captain;
     19: return
```

Let's understand the instructions:

- **new** allocates memory for the Captain object.

- **dup** duplicates the reference for the constructor call.

- **ldc** "INSTANCE" pushes the name of the enum constant (https://docs.oracle.com/javase/specs/jvms/se24/html/jvms-6.html#jvms-6.5.ldc).

- **iconst_0** pushes the ordinal value (0 for INSTANCE) (https://docs.oracle.com/javase/specs/jvms/se24/html/jvms-6.html#jvms-6.5.iconst_i).

- **invokespecial** calls the private constructor of Captain (https://docs.oracle.com/javase/specs/jvms/se24/html/jvms-6.html#jvms-6.5.invokespecial).

- **putstatic #3** assigns the newly created object to the static field INSTANCE (https://docs.oracle.com/javase/specs/jvms/se24/html/jvms-6.html#jvms-6.5.putstatic).

Effectively, at the source level, this corresponds to something like

```
INSTANCE = new Captain("INSTANCE", 0);
```

Q2.9 Why do we see 0 in the line: "INSTANCE = new Captain("INSTANCE", 0);"?

In an enum declaration, each constant is automatically assigned an ordinal value by the Java compiler. The ordinal represents the position of the constant within the enum declaration, starting from 0. For example:

```
public enum Captain {
    INSTANCE;
    // The remaining code is not shown
}
```

Here, INSTANCE is the first and only constant, so its ordinal is 0. However, if you had declared:

```
public enum Captain {
    INSTANCE, VICE_CAPTAIN;
    // Some other code, if any
}
```

Then the compiler would assign ordinals 0 and 1, respectively. You can verify this by examining the compiled bytecode using javap -c.

Q2.10 What are some common real-world use cases of the Singleton pattern?

Here are some common use cases where you'll find this pattern useful:

- To coordinate access to a centralized system, such as a database or configuration service

- To maintain a common log file

- To maintain a thread pool in a multithreaded environment

- To implement a caching mechanism or device drivers

Q2.11 What are the primary drawbacks (or critiques) of using the Singleton pattern?

Here are some common concerns:

- It promotes tight coupling and hidden dependencies. Why? Since this pattern uses global states, any part of the system can access them. As a result, several classes may become indirectly dependent on the same global instance, making testing and maintenance more difficult.

- It discourages subclassing, which is a common practice in object-oriented programming.

- The Singleton class violates the Single Responsibility Principle (SRP). Why? It manages both its business logic and its own lifecycle (it typically lives until the program terminates).

- Mocking a Singleton instance is difficult. Why? The instance itself manages its lifecycle.

- "Performance vs. laziness" is a recurring concern. Why? The developers often debate the trade-offs between synchronization, thread safety, and initialization strategy.

- Modern frameworks, which provide built-in dependency management, have also questioned the continuing usefulness of this pattern.

Q2.9 Given these drawbacks, I'd like to know your thoughts on those.

I believe that no pattern is inherently good or bad. **The key lies in how it is implemented.** However, I learned from my seniors that if the Singleton class contains mutable state, it can negatively affect an application. In other words, it signals a poor Singleton design.

Still, I believe that despite its flaws, the pattern retains its usefulness in certain scenarios (e.g., thread pools, logging utilities, or truly immutable configurations).

I remind you that your goal is to build high-quality software, not to blindly follow—or reject—a pattern or principle. For me, despite its controversies, the Singleton pattern continues to hold relevance in modern software design. The key lies not in rejecting it outright, but in using it judiciously—only when a single, shared instance truly makes sense.

Finally, I'd also like you to visit the following link:

https://www.informit.com/articles/article.aspx?p=1404056&lang=en

which features an insightful remark from Erich Gamma in a 2009 interview:

When discussing which patterns to drop, we found that we still love them all. (Not really—I'm in favor of dropping Singleton. Its use is almost always a design smell.)

I believe that this quote remains relevant in 2026 as well!

Summary

As said before, there are many approaches for modeling a singleton design pattern. In this chapter, you learned four different ways to implement the Singleton pattern. Each approach has its own merits and trade-offs:

- The **lazy initialization (with synchronization)** ensures controlled access but may have a slight performance overhead.

- The **eager initialization** is simple but lacks flexibility because the instance is created even if never used.

- **Bill Pugh's approach** (third one) is often preferred because it combines lazy initialization, thread safety, and simplicity without synchronization overhead.

- The **enum-based approach** (fourth one) offers the simplest syntax and built-in thread safety, but it is less flexible when inheritance or complex business logic is required.

Hopefully, these various implementations helped you understand how the Singleton pattern works, its variations, and where it fits best in modern Java development. However, I acknowledge that there is no single "best" implementation—it depends on your design goals. You understand that as a developer, you need to balance the clarity, performance, and thread safety in your application.

CHAPTER 3

Builder Pattern

The Builder pattern is useful for creating complex objects that have multiple fields, some of which may be optional. Instead of relying on long or overloaded constructors, the Builder pattern lets you construct an object step by step and produce a fully initialized instance at the end. This chapter explains this pattern using multiple examples.

Concept

The Gang of Four (GoF) defined the intent of this pattern as follows:

> *Separate the construction of a complex object from its representation so that the same construction process can create different representations.*

Here, "representation" denotes the final form of the object that you'd like to create. For example, a car builder can follow the same construction steps to produce a regular car (e.g., a petrol or a diesel car) or an electric car.

This pattern may be difficult to understand on the first attempt. Why? While constructing an object, you normally see the construction logic in the class. You also follow a single-step creation process (e.g., invoking a

© Vaskaran Sarcar 2026
V. Sarcar, *Creational Design Patterns in Java*, Apress Pocket Guides,
https://doi.org/10.1007/979-8-8688-2314-5_3

constructor with the required parameters) to construct the target object. **However, the Builder pattern tries to make you familiar with an alternative approach that has the following characteristics:**

- You see a configurable sequence of steps to make a complex object.

- You move the construction logic outside the class.

- You can reuse a specific process to build different products.

Now you ask: **How does it help?** Consider a typical case where you try to instantiate a complex object that has many parts, but you need to acquire the parameters for the constructor gradually and in a correct sequence. Probably, you have seen this while involved in parsing or dealing with a typical user interface. In fact, in our everyday life, you see similar applications. For example, while building a house, you first acquire the land, make the structure as per the plan, and then you add the luxuries.

Let's discuss about the coding. According to the classical GoF book, four key participants are involved in this pattern. Let me summarize their roles as follows:

- **Product**: It is a complex object that has many parts. In this chapter, you are about to construct cars using this pattern.

- **Builder**: It provides an abstract interface for creating parts of the complex object, i.e., the Product object.

- **ConcreteBuilder**: By implementing the Builder interface, it creates and assembles different parts of the product and provides an interface for retrieving it.

- **Director**: It constructs the object using the Builder interface.

Let me clear the roles using the following examples.

Real-Life Example

A car manufacturing company can produce different representations of a car, such as regular cars (a.k.a. traditional cars) and electric cars. It manufactures different parts of these cars and later assembles those parts as per the model's specifications. You know that this is a complex process. In addition, these parts are specific to the type of vehicle. So, the company can make two units, say a regular car builder unit and an electric car builder unit, to make these cars. Since these two units work differently, it is no wonder that a regular car looks different from an electric car. Finally, there must be someone who can supervise the overall process and instruct the units on how to make the cars. In this example, you can consider a car as the final Product, each car builder unit as a ConcreteBuilder, and the company supervisor as the Director. The Builder corresponds to the general set of steps or the standard procedure that every car builder unit must follow.

Let's consider another example. To complete an order for a computer, different hardware parts can be assembled based on customer preferences. For example, a customer can opt for a 1TB hard disk with an Intel processor. If there is a budget constraint, another customer can choose a 500GB hard disk with an AMD processor. Here, the computer is the final Product, the customer plays the role of the Director, the seller/assembler plays the role of the ConcreteBuilder, and the Builder is the common interface that all such assemblers follow.

Computer World Example

The classical GoF book considers an example when a typical application tries to convert one text format to another text format, such as converting from Rich Text Format (RTF) to ASCII text. A similar example is very common when you see online converters convert a Word (.docx) document to a PDF file (.pdf) or a plain text (.txt).

While programming similar examples, at a high level, you can think of a reader and a converter—for example, a Word doc reader and a format converter—where the reader parses the document and the converter converts it to a target format using a specialized converter. So, the converter can have specialized subclasses, such as a PDF converter or a TXT converter, to perform these conversions. In this example, the converter plays the role of a Builder, the specialized converters (such as PDF Converters or TXT Converters) play the role of ConcreteBuilder, the Word doc reader plays the role of a Director, and a converted file (such as .PDF or .TXT) is the final Product.

These examples give you a clue when to use the Builder pattern. Let me summarize the points now:

- You'd like to create a complex object that has many parts.

- Constructions of these parts are independent of each other.

- Constructions of these parts are also independent of how they are assembled.

There is one more point. The GoF also suggests that this pattern is useful

- When the construction process allows you to create different representations of the object (as explained earlier).

The First Implementation

In our upcoming example, you are about to create different cars. So, the Car class represents the Product. The Builder class defines all possible methods to construct a car. The ElectricCarBuilder and RegularCarBuilder are concrete classes that inherit from this Builder class. The Director class plays the role of the manufacturer and orchestrates the construction process.

Explicit Director

In this implementation, the client creates a Director object and configures it with a Builder object to make the cars. The director uses a RegularCarBuilder instance to construct and assemble parts of a regular car. Similarly, the director uses an ElectricCarBuilder instance to construct an electric car.

As said before, in our example, the **Car** is the complex object under consideration, which can have different representations (electric and regular cars). This class has the following look:

POINT TO NOTE

Since this product class (Car.java) is used in all the demonstrations in this chapter, I have placed it inside the builder.product package to avoid code duplication.

// Car.java

```java
package builder.product;

// The Car class represents the "Product"
public class Car {
    private String type;
    private int seats;
    private String motor;
    // The exhaust emission is not needed for an electric car
    private boolean exhaustEmissionSystem;

    public void setExhaustEmissionSystem(boolean exhaustEmissionSystem) {
      this.exhaustEmissionSystem = exhaustEmissionSystem;
    }
```

```java
  public void setType(String type) {
   this.type = type;
  }
  public void setSeats(int seats) {
   this.seats = seats;
  }
  public void setMotor(String motor) {
   this.motor = motor;
  }
  @Override
  public String toString() {
   StringBuilder sb = new StringBuilder();
   sb.append("\n type=").append(type).append(",")
     .append("\n seats=").append(seats).append(",")
     .append("\n motor=").append(motor).append(",")
     .append("\n exhaustEmissionSystem=").append(exhaustEmissionSystem);
   return sb.toString();
  }
}
```

Typically, a builder interface is needed for creating parts of a Product object. In our example, **Builder** is an abstract class that plays this role. It contains separate methods to build different parts of a product.

POINT TO NOTE

In this example, you see an empty method called addExhaustSystem in the Builder class. Why? Ideally, this class should define all possible methods to build various parts of a product (in our example, a car). We can assume that an electric car does not need an exhaust emission system, whereas a regular car must have such a component. I could make other methods in the Builder class empty as well; however, I forced the concrete builders to provide the implementations for those methods. This approach allows subclasses to override the addExhaustSystem() method only when it is absolutely required. **This is nothing but a design decision.** There is another viewpoint: if every subclass is expected to provide its own implementation, then making the method abstract is the better choice because it forces subclasses to override it.

In short, both approaches are correct depending on the expected number of subclasses and how many of them need custom logic—something that cannot always be predicted, as real systems evolve.

Let's have a look at this class:

```java
// Builder.java

package builder.demo1;

import builder.product.Car;

public abstract class Builder {
    public abstract void createEmptyCar();
    public abstract void setCarType();
    public abstract void setSeats();
    public abstract void setMotor();
    // The exhaust emission system may not be needed for all cars
    public void addExhaustSystem() {
    }
```

```
  // To retrieve the constructed product.
  public abstract Car getCar();
}
```

Author's note: You may note that the getCar() method will be used to retrieve the finished product after the parts are assembled. Shortly, you'll see the Director class as well. The Director's buildCar() method will use this getCar() method to return the constructed object.

The **RegularCarBuilder** class and the **ElectricCarBuilder** class inherit from the Builder class, providing the necessary methods to construct and assemble the parts. You understand that these concrete builders build the internal representations of a Car instance. First, see the **ElectricCarBuilder** class:

// ElectricCarBuilder.java

```
package builder.demo1;

import builder.product.Car;

public class ElectricCarBuilder extends Builder {
  private Car car;
  @Override
  public void createEmptyCar() {
    car = new Car();
  }
  @Override
  public void setCarType() {
    car.setType("Electric");
  }
  @Override
  public void setMotor() {
    car.setMotor("electric motors and batteries");
  }
```

```java
    @Override
    public void setSeats() {
     car.setSeats(4);
    }
    @Override
    public Car getCar() {
     return car;
    }

    // NOTE: The exhaust emission system is not needed
    // for the electric cars. So, we do not touch the
    // empty implementation of the parent class (Builder)
}
```

Now see the RegularCarBuilder class (notice that it overrides the addExhaustSystem() method as well):

// RegularCarBuilder.java

```java
package builder.demo1;

import builder.product.Car;

public class RegularCarBuilder extends Builder {
    private Car car;
    @Override
    public void createEmptyCar() {
       car = new Car();
    }
    @Override
    public void setCarType() {
     car.setType("Regular");
    }
```

```java
  @Override
  public void setMotor() {
    car.setMotor("internal combustion engine (fueled by diesel)");
  }
  // The exhaust emission system is needed for regular cars
  @Override
  public void addExhaustSystem() {
    car.setExhaustEmissionSystem(true);
  }
  @Override
  public void setSeats() {
   car.setSeats(5);
  }
  @Override
  public Car getCar() {
   return car;
  }
}
```

The **Director** is responsible for creating the final object using the appropriate builder. **It is important to note that the director is the one who decides the sequence of steps to build the product**. You can safely assume that directors can vary the sequence as they wish. Here is the Director class:

// Director.java

```java
package builder.demo1;

import builder.product.Car;

// The director directs the steps to make the product (car).
public class Director {
    private Builder builder;
```

```
  public Director(Builder builder) {
    this.builder = builder;
  }

  // The director performs the steps in the following sequence and returns the
  // constructed product: create empty car->set car type-> set motor-> set seats->
  // add exhaust system(if applicable)
  public Car buildCar() {
      builder.createEmptyCar(); // Always start with a new car
      builder.setCarType();
      builder.setMotor();
      builder.setSeats();
      builder.addExhaustSystem();
      return builder.getCar();
  }
  public void setBuilder(Builder builder) {
    this.builder=builder;
  }
}
}
```

You have seen the key players of the Builder pattern. Now let me show you the class diagram (Figure 3-1) before you see the client code (**BPDemo1Client.java**).

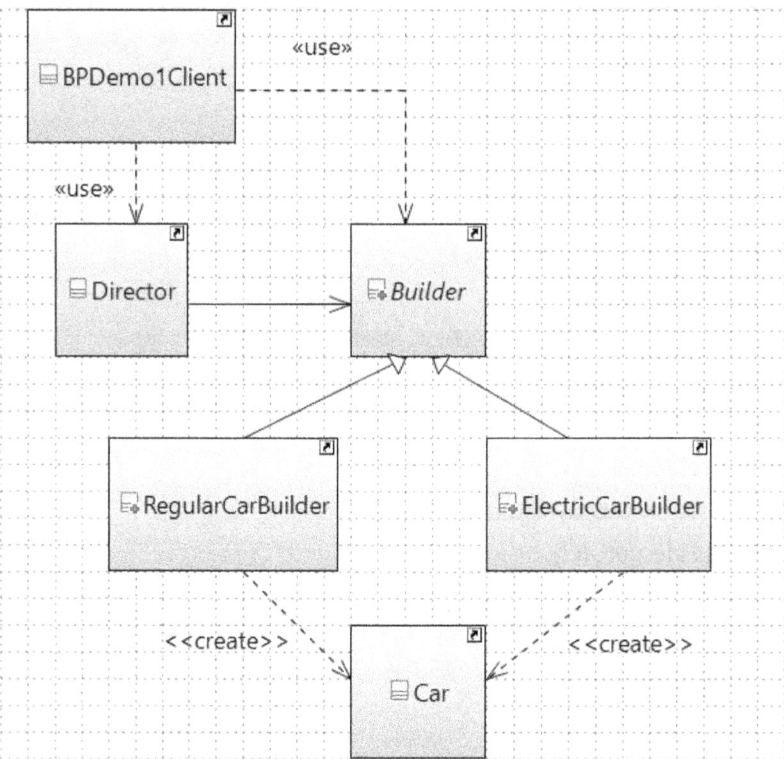

Figure 3-1. *Following the Builder pattern, the Director and Builders collaborate to construct the final products (Regular and Electric Cars) in Demonstration 1*

Demonstration 1

Let's allow a client to make some cars now.

POINT TO NOTE

Similar to previous chapters, in all demonstrations in this chapter, only the client classes are kept package-private. All other classes—such as the Builder, its concrete implementations, the Product, and the optional Director—are intentionally declared public. Keeping the client package-private ensures that it remains an internal entry point for the examples, while the public classes represent the reusable and extensible parts of the Builder pattern.

// BPDemo1Client.java

```java
package builder.demo1.client;

import builder.demo1.Builder;
import builder.demo1.Director;
import builder.demo1.ElectricCarBuilder;
import builder.demo1.RegularCarBuilder;
import builder.product.Car;

class BPDemo1Client {
    public static void main(String[] args) {
        System.out.println("*** Builder Pattern Demonstration.***\n");
        // Making a regular car
        Builder builder = new RegularCarBuilder();
        Director director = new Director(builder);
        Car car = director.buildCar();
        System.out.println("The car details:"+ car);

        System.out.println("============");

        // Making an electric car now.
        builder = new ElectricCarBuilder();
        director.setBuilder(builder);
```

```java
    car = director.buildCar();
    System.out.println("The car details:"+ car);
    System.out.println("============");
  }
}
```

Output

Here is the output:

*** Builder Pattern Demonstration.***

The car details:
 type=Regular,
 seats=5,
 motor=internal combustion engine (fueled by diesel),
 exhaustEmissionSystem=true
============
The car details:
 type=Electric,
 seats=4,
 motor=electric motors and batteries,
 exhaustEmissionSystem=false
============

Q&A Session

Q3.1 What is the advantage of using a builder pattern?

Here are some advantages:

- You direct the builder to build the objects step-by-step, and you promote encapsulation by hiding the details of the complex construction process. The director can retrieve the final product from the builder when the whole construction is over. In general, at a high level, you seem to have only one method that makes the product, but other internal methods are hidden from the client. So, you have **finer control over the construction process**.

- Using this pattern, the same construction process can produce different products. You have seen that by changing the type of a builder, you change the internal representation of the product.

- Most importantly, notice that if you need to build sports cars in the future, you can add an appropriate concrete builder, say SportsCarBuilder, that can implement the methods defined in the Builder class as per its needs. While doing this, you typically do not need to make any changes in the Car, Builder, or the existing concrete builder classes.

Author's note: The previous statement holds as long as the structure of the Car remains the same. If the Car class changes (e.g., if fields are added or removed), the Builder interface and its concrete implementations—and possibly the Director—must be updated accordingly.

POINT TO NOTE

Typically, the use of a constructor or a method that takes too many parameters is often discouraged. While using them, you need to pass those parameters in the correct order, which increases the chance of errors. The situation becomes even more error-prone when multiple parameters share the same (or similar) type.

Q3.2 What are the drawbacks associated with a builder pattern?

Here are some challenges:

- It adds extra complexity and code because you must create additional Builder classes.

- Some initialization logic may be duplicated between builders, which can introduce maintenance overhead.

- If the number of product variations grows, you may need more concrete builders, which can lead to a potential class explosion.

Q3.3 Why are you using a separate class for the director? You could use the client code to play the role of the director. Is this correct?

No one restricts you from doing that. I wanted to separate this role from the client code in this implementation. In Demonstration 2, I'll make the client a director.

Q3.4 I have read your other book, *Design Patterns in Java (Third Edition)*.[1] In that book, you used specialized directors and specialized products as well. However, in this example, you used only specialized builders. Is there any specific thought behind this?

That is a fat book with a detailed discussion on many different topics. Yes, by making a common class (or interface) for specialized products and a common class (or interface) for specialized directors, you can make a bigger system. However, this is a pocketbook. To make the example simple, I have shown you this concise implementation. In addition, the GoF shared their thoughts as follows:

> *Why no abstract class for products? In the common case, the products produced by the concrete builders differ so greatly in their representation that there is little to gain from giving different products a common parent class.*

---

[1] https://link.springer.com/book/10.1007/978-1-4842-7971-7

You can also justify this quote by looking at the output of Demonstration 1, where a regular car is very much different from an electric car.

Q3.5 Does the Builder pattern promote OCP?

The builder pattern is extension-friendly. As said before, consider a case when you'd also like to make sports cars. In this case, you can use an appropriate concrete builder, say SportsCarBuilder, that can implement the methods defined in the Builder class as per its needs. While doing this, you do not need to make any changes in the product (Car class) or the existing builders. This means these are closed for modifications.

However, if you'd like to add a new build step (e.g., addAirConditioner()), you end up modifying the base class (Builder) and all its concrete implementations. In that case, the pattern does not strictly follow the OCP.

Q3.6 If I involve more specialized directors, they can follow a different sequence of steps. Is this correct?

Yes. It is a good find. However, by slightly updating Demonstration 1, you can vary the construction steps as well. How? You can customize the build sequence by adding new methods to the Director. For example, the following method in the Director class can create cars without seats:

```
public Car buildCarWithoutSeats() {
        builder.createEmptyCar(); // Always start with a new car
        builder.setCarType();
        builder.setMotor();
        //builder.setSeats(); // not setting seats any more
        builder.addExhaustSystem();
        return builder.getCar();

}
```

You'll shortly see that the upcoming demonstration (Demonstration 2) is more flexible. That demonstration will use method chaining to vary the steps inside the client code. **However, this added flexibility does not mean Demonstration 1 is inferior.** In Demonstration 1, the Director hides the construction sequence from the client, so the client does not need to know the order of construction or details. **This promotes better encapsulation and reduces the chance of incorrect construction.**

Alternative Implementations

Let's see an alternative implementation using method chaining now.

Fluent Builder

In this program, **the client plays the role of a director**. So, I need to incorporate some changes in the previous demonstration. Let's understand these changes.

Note   As mentioned earlier, the Car class is reused from the **builder. product** package in this demonstration. You can find all other classes in this example in the builder.demo2 package.

Similar to the previous example, the Builder class still represents the builder interface. However, the methods are updated so that instead of returning void, they now return the Builder itself. This enables **method chaining**, as shown below:

```
package builder.demo2;

import builder.product.Car;
```

```java
public abstract class Builder {
    public abstract Builder createEmptyCar();
    public abstract Builder setCarType();
    public abstract Builder setSeats();
    public abstract Builder setMotor();
    // The exhaust emission system may not be needed for all cars
    public Builder addExhaustSystem() {
     return this;
    }
    // To retrieve the constructed product.
    public abstract Car getCar();
}
```

As a result, the inherited classes of the Builder class (RegularCarBuilder and ElectricCarBuilder) also need to adjust to the changes. First, see the RegularCarBuilder class with the key changes in bold:

```java
// RegularCarBuilder.java
package builder.demo2;

import builder.product.Car;

public class RegularCarBuilder extends Builder {
    private Car car;
    @Override
    public Builder createEmptyCar() {
      car = new Car();
      return this;
    }
    @Override
    public Builder setCarType() {
      car.setType("Regular");
      return this;
    }
```

```java
@Override
public Builder setMotor() {
   car.setMotor("internal combustion engine (fueled by diesel)");
   return this;
}

// The exhaust emission system is needed for regular cars
@Override
public Builder addExhaustSystem() {
  car.setExhaustEmissionSystem(true);
  return this;
}
@Override
public Builder setSeats() {
   car.setSeats(5);
   return this;
}
@Override
 public Car getCar() {
   return car;
}
}
}
```

POINT TO NOTE

These methods are similar to the previous demonstration, but their return type is **Builder** now. As a result, now a client can apply **method chaining** to assemble the parts.

The ElectricCarBuilder class makes similar changes. To avoid repetition, I do not show it here. You may also remember that the addExhaustSystem() method is already defined in the parent Builder class and does not need to be overridden for an electric car.

Let me show you the updated class diagram (Figure 3-2) before you see the client code (**BPDemo2Client.java**).

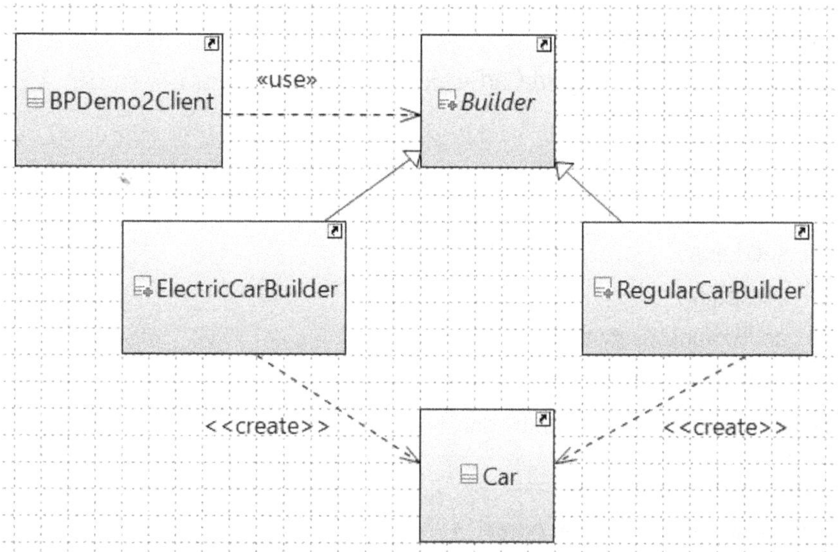

Figure 3-2. *The client (as a director) directly uses the RegularCarBuilder to create regular cars and the ElectricCarBuilder to create electric cars in Demonstration 2*

Demonstration 2

Let's see how a client can vary the steps to make different products in the following example:

// BPDemo2Client.java

```java
package builder.demo2.client;

import builder.demo2.Builder;
import builder.demo2.ElectricCarBuilder;
import builder.demo2.RegularCarBuilder;
import builder.product.Car;
```

```java
class BPDemo2Client {
  public static void main(String[] args) {
     System.out.println("*** Builder Pattern Demonstration.***\n");
     // Making a regular car
     Builder builder = new RegularCarBuilder();
     Car car = builder
         .createEmptyCar()
         .setCarType()
         .setMotor()
         .setSeats()
         .addExhaustSystem()
         .getCar();
     System.out.println("The car details:"+ car);

     System.out.println("===========");
       // Making an electric car now.
       // Following the different sequence (setting the motor before the seats)
       builder = new ElectricCarBuilder();
       car = builder
         .createEmptyCar()
         .setCarType()
         .setSeats() // Making seats before setting the motor now
         .setMotor()
         .getCar();
     System.out.println("The car details:"+ car);

     System.out.println("===========");
     }
}
```

Output

Let's verify the output now:

```
*** Builder Pattern Demonstration.***

The car details:
 type=Regular,
 seats=5,
 motor=internal combustion engine (fueled by diesel),
 exhaustEmissionSystem=true
============
The car details:
 type=Electric,
 seats=4,
 motor=electric motors and batteries,
 exhaustEmissionSystem=false
============
```

Analysis

Although the outputs of Demonstration 1 and Demonstration 2 happen to be identical, observe the difference in the construction sequence. In this program (Demonstration 2), while building an electric car, the client (a.k.a. director) sets the seats before setting the motor. In contrast, while building the regular car, the sequence is different—the motor was set before the seats. **Now you understand that this approach provides more flexibility while making an application.**

You may also note that the builders in both demonstrations apply the same set of values to the car (same type, same motor, same seat count, and the same exhaust-system). Since the **toString**() method prints only the **final state** of the car but not the order in which the values were set, these outputs seem to be identical.

POINT TO NOTE

In both demonstrations, the set (or create) methods to construct an object are defined by the Builder interface. In Demonstration 1, the Director defines the sequence of methods to construct the object, while in Demonstration 2, the client defines the sequence (same or different order). Introducing parameterized builder methods can make the construction process even more dynamic, giving the client or director flexibility without changing the builder classes. **Demonstration 3** illustrates this idea when I modify the **setSeats** builder method to accept an **int** parameter.

Q&A Session

Q3.7 Looks like you promoted functional programming and immutability in Demonstration 2. Is this correct?

Good catch. I must say that you are an excellent reader. The void methods often modify the internal state of an existing object, which goes against immutability. Functional programming discourages such side-effect-producing operations because they make code harder to reason about. In contrast, in demonstration 2, our builder uses method chaining, where each method returns the Builder itself. This fluent style allows operations to be composed like functions—reflecting a functional-programming influence in the code.

Author's note: Functional programming (FP) is a big topic. A detailed discussion on FP is beyond the scope of this book. However, I have written a book on functional programming using C#. If interested, you can refer to the book *Introducing Functional Programming Using C#.*[2]

---

[2] https://link.springer.com/book/10.1007/978-1-4842-9697-4

Q3.8 What is the key benefit associated with immutable objects?

Once created, the state of an immutable object never changes. As a result, these objects are naturally thread-safe. Therefore, while using them, you can save lots of synchronization costs in a multithreaded environment.

Q3.9 Earlier, you warned me that a constructor (or a method) with too many parameters is often discouraged. Can you discuss this further?

Consider the following code snippet:

```
class A {
   A(int arg1, int arg2, int arg3, double arg4, B b, C c) {
      // Some code to initialize
   }
   // Remaining code skipped
}
class B { }
class C { }
```

Let's analyze the potential difficulties:

- **Dependency creation:** Notice that the B and C objects are part of an A object. So, before constructing an instance of A, you must explicitly create B and C. This adds extra steps and coupling, making the process less straightforward.

- **Parameter overload:** The constructor also requires three integers and a double. Since the parameters are similar (arg1, arg2, arg3), their purpose is not self-explanatory. Without documentation, it's hard to understand what each represents, and even small mistakes in the order of arguments can lead to bugs.

- **Maintainability issues:** As the class grows, adding more parameters will only increase the complexity and make the code harder to use and maintain.

These are some typical reasons—methods or constructors with too many parameters are generally **not recommended.** A better practice is to keep the number of parameters minimal (ideally, no more than two at a time).

Moreover, in many cases, not all configuration options are needed. For example, you saw that an electric car did not require an "exhaust emission system." It is better if clients are not forced to pass arguments that are irrelevant in certain contexts.

You understand that in such situations, the Builder pattern can help. It allows you to construct complex objects step by step, improves readability, reduces errors, and makes the code more flexible to future changes.

Q3.10 Can you give me a built-in example of the Builder pattern?

You can consider java.lang.StringBuilder class is a **close example** in this context. But you need to remember that the GoF definition also states that this pattern allows use the same construction process to create different representations of a product. In this context, this example does not fully qualify the GoF's definition.

However, I'd like you to note that the java.util.Calendar.Builder class is an example in this category. But it is available from Java 8 onward only. Here is a sample usage:

```
Calendar calender= new Calendar.Builder()
    .setCalendarType("gregory")    // choose calendar type
    .setTimeZone(TimeZone.getTimeZone("GMT+05:30")) // IST offset
    .setDate(2025, 8, 12)      // set date (month is 0-based: 8 = September)
    .setTimeOfDay(9, 30, 0)   // set time of day
    .build(); // creates the final Calender object
```

Q3.11 It appears that the Builder pattern is similar to the Factory pattern. Is this correct?

In the Factory patterns, you focused on a one-step creation process. However, you use the Builder pattern when you see a configurable sequence of steps.

POINT TO NOTE

In the future, you may like to learn about the Template method pattern. In that case, I'd like you to note that in the Builder pattern, the client/customer is the boss (you have already seen the client as a director in Demonstration 2) who controls the order of the algorithm. On the contrary, in the Template Method pattern, you (or the developers) are the boss, and you have absolute control over the flow of the execution, which cannot be altered by a client.

Refactoring

The previous implementations followed the classical Builder pattern. **In those implementations, the abstract builder does not know anything significant about the product.** You can now employ a small refinement to those implementations. At first look, it may appear that this refinement may slightly deviate from the GoF's intent, where the abstract builder was responsible only for providing an interface for creating the parts of the product (e.g., cars in our example), and the concrete builders assemble the parts and provide an interface for retrieving the product. Still, I'd propose the following changes:

REMINDER

When we say "program to an interface," we are not referring strictly to a Java interface. The term simply means "program to a supertype." This supertype can be an abstract class, a superclass, or even a Java interface (possibly with default methods)—anything that defines the construction contract.

First, if you analyze the implementations, you can discover that there are certain repetitions. For example, the createEmptyCar and getCar methods have **identical implementations** inside the concrete builders. Are the repetitions good? No. By following the DRY (Don't Repeat Yourself) principle, you can eliminate those repetitions from our earlier implementations.

Author's note: Andy Hunt and Dave Thomas wrote about the DRY principle in their book *The Pragmatic Programmer* (First Edition, October 1999). The DRY principle is stated as follows: **Every piece of knowledge must have a single, unambiguous, authoritative representation within a system.** If interested, you can see a detailed discussion on it in my other C# book *Simple and Efficient Programming with C# (Second Edition)*.

Next, I told you that introducing parameterized builder methods can make the construction process even more dynamic, and sometimes, it is necessary as well. To illustrate, let's assume that while building the cars, the client would like to decide the number of seats in this car. How do we adopt this idea? You guessed it right—the setSeats builder method can accept an int parameter to fulfill this need.

Keeping these points in mind, let's look at the following code, with the key changes in bold. I have also kept the supporting comments for your easy understanding:

Note   As mentioned earlier, the Car class is reused from the **builder. product** package in this demonstration. You can find all other classes in this example in the **builder.demo3** package.

```java
// Builder.java
package builder.demo3;

import builder.product.Car;

public abstract class Builder {

    // The createEmptyCar and getCar method implementations
    // are common in concrete builders in this implementation.
    // So, those are placed here. (The car variable is protected now)

    protected Car car;
    public Builder createEmptyCar() {
      car = new Car();
      return this;
    }
    public abstract Builder setCarType();
    // This method accepts a parameter now
    public abstract Builder setSeats(int seatCount);
    public abstract Builder setMotor();
    // The exhaust emission system may not be needed for all cars
    public Builder addExhaustSystem() {
      return this;
    }
    // To retrieve the constructed product. It is not abstract now.
    public Car getCar() {
      return car;
    }
}
```

The concrete builders have become very concise now. Here is one of them:

```java
// RegularCarBuilder.java
package builder.demo3;

public class RegularCarBuilder extends Builder {

  @Override
  public Builder setCarType() {
   car.setType("Regular");
   return this;
  }
  @Override
  public Builder setMotor() {
   car.setMotor("internal combustion engine (fueled by diesel)");
   return this;
  }
  // The exhaust emission system is needed for regular cars
  @Override
  public Builder addExhaustSystem() {
   car.setExhaustEmissionSystem(true);
   return this;
  }
  @Override
  public Builder setSeats(int seatCount) {
   car.setSeats(seatCount);
   return this;
  }
}
```

The other concrete builder is also concise now. Since it is not very big, let's have a look at it as well:

```java
// ElectricCarBuilder.java
package builder.demo3;

public class ElectricCarBuilder extends Builder {
  @Override
  public Builder  setCarType() {
    car.setType("Electric");
    return this;
  }

  @Override
  public Builder setMotor() {
    car.setMotor("electric motors and batteries");
    return this;
  }
  @Override
  public Builder setSeats(int seatCount) {
    car.setSeats(seatCount);
    return this;
  }

  // NOTE: The exhaust emission system is not needed
  // for the electric cars. So, we do not touch the
  // empty implementation of the parent class (Builder)
}
```

Note   Since the Car class is reused, I'll not repeat it here. You can see the complete implementation in the **builder.demo3** package.

Demonstration 3

Let's see the client class now (see the key changes in bold):

// BPDemo3Client.java

```
package builder.demo3.client;

import builder.demo3.Builder;
import builder.demo3.ElectricCarBuilder;
import builder.demo3.RegularCarBuilder;
import builder.product.Car;

class BPDemo3Client {
  public static void main(String[] args) {
  System.out.println("*** Builder Pattern Demonstration.***\n");
    // Making a regular car
    Builder builder = new RegularCarBuilder();
    Car car = builder
    .createEmptyCar()
    .setCarType()
    .setMotor()
    .setSeats(5)
    .addExhaustSystem()
    .getCar();
    System.out.println("The car details:"+ car);
    System.out.println("============");

    // Making an electric car now.
    // Following the different sequence (setting the motor before the seats)
    builder = new ElectricCarBuilder();
    car = builder
    .createEmptyCar()
    .setCarType()
```

```
    .setSeats(4)
    .setMotor()
    .getCar();
    System.out.println("The car details:"+ car);
    System.out.println("============");
  }
}
```

Output

Since I passed the same number of seats (5 for the regular car and 4 for the electric car), there is no surprise that the output is identical to the previous demonstrations. Hence, it is not repeated here.

Analysis

In our earlier demonstrations, the abstract builder contained an empty implementation of addExhaustSystem(). In this demonstration (Demonstration 3), we have extended this idea further by moving more shared functionality into the abstract builder, making the concrete builders even more concise. **Finally, introducing a parameterized builder method, we made the construction process even more dynamic.**

However, now the abstract builder **hard-codes the product type** (Car). So, if tomorrow, you'd like to use a **product hierarchy** (where Car is an interface and you derive RegularCar and ElectricCar from it), you need to revert the design. It is because the abstract builder cannot know which one to instantiate. In this case, only the **concrete builders** know which specific product variant they are supposed to build.

This is why Demonstration 3 works only if there's a **single product class** (or a very stable product structure). Otherwise, it becomes restrictive. However, the idea of using a parameterized builder method is undoubtedly promising.

Summary

This chapter showed you three different implementations to demonstrate the Builder pattern. In the first example, you saw an explicit director. In the next example, the client plays the director's role. Here you learned about the fluent builder. In the final example, we refactored the code to remove code duplications and discussed the pros and cons.

Prototype Pattern

The Prototype pattern provides an alternative method for instantiating an object by copying (or cloning) an instance of an existing object. This chapter explains this pattern and its usefulness with simple examples.

Concept

The Gang of Four (GoF) defined the intent of the Prototype pattern as follows:

> *Specify the kinds of objects to create using a prototypical instance, and create new objects by copying this prototype.*

You can see that the core idea of this pattern is to create a new object from an existing one. In other words, the existing object serves as a template for the new object. You may wonder: *How does cloning help?* The answer lies in efficiency. Cloning can significantly reduce both time and cost in certain scenarios. Here are some examples:

- Your intended object requires resources that are complex or difficult to obtain.

- You recognize that building a new object from scratch involves a lengthy or expensive initialization process.

© Vaskaran Sarcar 2026
V. Sarcar, *Creational Design Patterns in Java*, Apress Pocket Guides,
https://doi.org/10.1007/979-8-8688-2314-5_4

Real-Life Example

Suppose you have a master copy of a valuable document. You need to make some modifications to analyze the effects. Instead of altering the original, you create a photocopy of the document and apply the changes to the copy. This way, the original remains intact while you experiment with the variation.

Computer World Example

Consider a scenario where you already have a stable application. Now, you want to enhance it with a new feature or test it with some minor changes. To fulfil the requirement, you can begin with a copy of the existing application, apply the changes, and then evaluate the outcome. Naturally, you would not want to rebuild the entire application from scratch just to verify those modifications, as that would waste both time and resources.

The clone() method of the Object class is a well-known example of the Prototype pattern. This method can create and return a copy of an existing object. However, while using it, there are certain important considerations. Let me highlight a few of them directly from the official Java documentation (Javadoc) for quick reference:

Note   To view the documentation, you can hover the cursor over the method name in Eclipse. Alternatively, you can consult the official documentation Object (Java SE 25 & JDK 25).[1]

- By convention, the returned object should be obtained by calling super.clone.

---

[1] https://docs.oracle.com/en/java/javase/25/docs/api/java.base/java/lang/Object.html#clone

- By convention, the object returned by this method should be independent of this object (which is being cloned). To achieve this independence, it may be necessary to modify one or more fields of the object returned by super.clone before returning it.

- Typically, this means copying any mutable objects that comprise the internal "deep structure" of the object being cloned and replacing the references to these objects with references to the copies. If a class contains only primitive fields or references to immutable objects, then it is usually the case that no fields in the object returned by super.clone need to be modified.

- If the object's class of this object does not implement the interface Cloneable, then the CloneNotSupportedException is thrown.

SHALLOW COPY VS. DEEP COPY

The official documentation (see the previous link) explicitly states that clone() performs a **shallow copy**, not a **deep copy**. If you are unfamiliar with these terms, let me tell you that they simply refer to two distinct cloning techniques. In the case of a **shallow copy**, the primitive (simple) fields of a class are duplicated in the cloned instance. However, for reference-type fields, only the references are copied—not the actual objects they point to. As a result, both the original and the cloned instances share references to the same objects. This can lead to unexpected issues; for example, an update in one object may reflect the changes in the other object (and vice versa). To avoid such problems, a **deep copy** is required. In a deep copy, not only the primitive fields but also the referenced objects are fully duplicated, ensuring that the clone is entirely independent of the original. **This also makes deep copying more expensive than performing a shallow copy**. In this chapter, you will see a more detailed discussion on these cloning techniques shortly.

The First Implementation

In Chapters 1 and 3, we constructed different types of cars using the **Factory Method** and **Builder** patterns. The **Prototype** pattern is often compared with these, so let us build cars once again using this pattern. This exercise will help you understand how different patterns can be applied to produce similar products. Before moving to the implementation, read the following paragraphs to avoid any future confusion.

Key Considerations

The Prototype design pattern can be implemented in multiple ways. Typically, you will see an abstract class (or an interface) acting as the abstract prototype. This abstract prototype defines a cloning method, which must be implemented by its concrete prototypes.

A client requests a prototype and modifies it as needed to create the desired object.

In many cases, a shallow copy is sufficient, but depending on the scenario, a deep copy mechanism may be necessary. **In the upcoming example, I will demonstrate a deep copy implementation.**

To keep the code concise, I will use only one concrete prototype— Ford.java—which extends the abstract prototype Car.java. Once you understand this example, you should be able to add more concrete prototypes without difficulty.

For the upcoming coding example, I assume that while purchasing a car, a customer is typically interested in the following details:

- The company that manufactured the car

- The price of the car (assumed here to be the on-road price)

- The model name and its color

For the first two, I have used the simple types String and double. For the model and color, however, I have introduced a user-defined type, Model. **Why is Model a user-defined type?** It'll help me to illustrate why and when a deep copy is required. Let me give you a clue: since Model is a user-defined type (a reference type), a shallow copy would only duplicate its reference, not the object itself. To handle this correctly, we need to implement a deep copy. Let's see the Model class now:

POINT TO NOTE

In this chapter, you will see two different implementations. Both implementations make use of the common files Model.java and Car.java, which are therefore placed in the package **prototype.common**.

```java
// Model. java
package prototype.common;

public class Model {
  public String modelName;
  public String color;

  public Model(String modelName, String color) {
    this.modelName = modelName;
    this.color = color;
  }
```

```
@Override
public String toString() {
    return modelName + ", Color:" + color;
  }
}
```

POINT TO NOTE

The fields in this class are declared as public solely to keep this Prototype pattern example simple and focused. In production code, these would typically be private with appropriate getters and setters.

I have provided the deep cloning implementation inside the abstract prototype Car.java, rather than in Ford.java. **Why is the cloning mechanism placed in the abstract class instead of its subclass?** This arrangement better serves the requirements of our example. Once you examine the implementation, the rationale will become clear.

POINTS TO NOTE

In my implementation, the client code will directly access the clone() method; therefore, I have declared it as public. Although the Model object is cloned as part of the deep copy, I intentionally reset the model and price-related fields after cloning (**this is an optional step for you**). This ensures that customer-specific attributes begin in a clean state for each new configuration, while company information remains unchanged. The company information is supplied in the derived class, Ford.java.

Below is the Car class, which contains the key method, clone (I have kept some comments for your better understanding):

// Car. java

```java
package prototype.common;

public abstract class Car implements Cloneable {
    protected Model model;
    protected double price;
    protected Car(Model model, double price) {
      this.model = model;
      this.price = price;
  }

    @Override
    public Car clone() throws CloneNotSupportedException {
      // First, making a shallow copy
      Car clonedCar = (Car) super.clone();
      // For a deep copy, manually instantiate all the reference type(s)
      // The following code will copy the existing model info as well.
      clonedCar.model = new Model(clonedCar.model.modelName, clonedCar.
        model.color);
      // Resetting customer-specific attributes so the cloned car
      // can be configured for a new customer, while company info remains unchanged
      clonedCar.resetModelAndPrice();
      return clonedCar;
  }
    protected void resetModelAndPrice() {
      // Resetting the model
      this.model = new Model("Not defined", "Not set");
      // Resetting the price as well
      this.price = 0;
  }
    public abstract void updateCar(String modelName, String color, double price);
}
```

The Ford class inherits from the Car class and overrides the required methods. Let's see this class:

// Ford. Java

```java
package prototype.demo1;

import prototype.common.Car;
import prototype.common.Model;

public class Ford extends Car {
  private String company;
  public Ford(Model model, double price) {
    super(model, price);
    company = "Ford";
  }
  @Override
  public void updateCar(String modelName, String color, double price) {
    this.model.modelName=modelName;
    this.model.color=color;
    this.price = price;
  }
  @Override
  public String toString() {
    return "Company:" + company + ", Model: " + model + ", Price:" + price + "\n";
  }
}
```

Now you are ready to examine the client code that demonstrates the following steps:

- First, I create a Ford-class instance. Then, I create another instance by cloning the previous instance.

- After that, I introduce some changes in the cloned copy and display the details. **A change in the cloned copy should not be reflected in the original copy (and vice versa).** So, I verify the effect of my changes.

- Finally, I test the reverse scenario, in which I make some changes in the initial car (from which the cloned car was built) and confirm that these changes do not reflect in the cloned car.

Before you see the client (PPDemo1Client.java), let me show you the following class diagram (Figure 4-1) to help you visualize the design of the application.

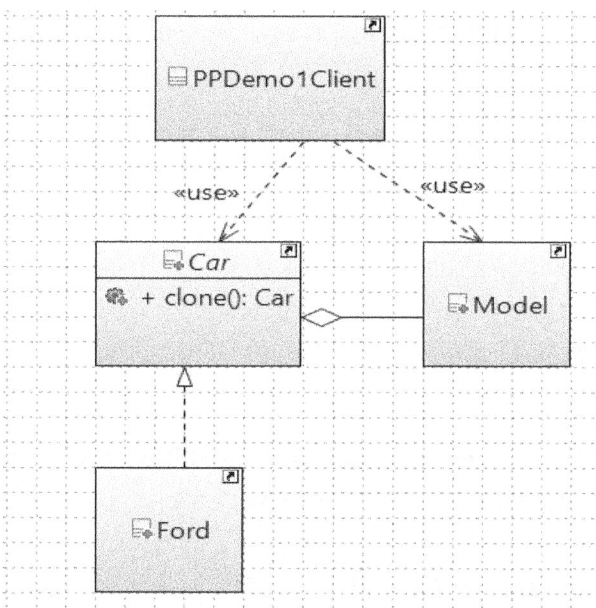

Figure 4-1. *The class diagram of the Prototype pattern implementation in Demonstration 1*

Author's note: In this program, the client first creates a Ford instance and supplies the model details through the constructor. After that, all new cars are created by cloning the existing instance rather than constructing them from scratch. This is why the diagram shows two "use" dependencies: one representing the constructor-based creation (for explicitly creating and passing a Model instance) and the other representing the cloning operation (dependency is on the abstraction (i.e., on the prototype)). Finally, for clarity, only the clone() method is shown to indicate the creation of a cloned object. Other attributes and methods are intentionally omitted to keep the diagram simple and consistent with the style used throughout this book.

Demonstration 1

You have already seen Model.Java, Car.Java, and Ford.Java. Now see the client code:

// PPDemo1Client.java

```java
package prototype.demo1.client;

import prototype.common.Model;
import prototype.common.Car;
import prototype.demo1.Ford;

class PPDemo1Client {
  public static void main(String[] args) throws CloneNotSupportedException {
    System.out.println("***Prototype Pattern Demo***\n");
    // Deciding a model
    Model model = new Model("Maverick", "Silver");
    // First, creating a Ford instance
    Car initialCar = new Ford(model, 25000);
    System.out.println("The initial car details:");
    System.out.println(initialCar);
```

```java
System.out.println("Getting another Ford car with some default settings by cloning.");
Car clonedCar = initialCar.clone();
System.out.println("The cloned car details:");
System.out.println(clonedCar);
System.out.println("==============================");

// Discussing the problem of shallow copy/ advantage of deep copy
System.out.println("Updating the cloned car now.");
clonedCar.updateCar("Ranger", "Blue", 40000);
System.out.println("\nVerifying the change effect on both cars...");
System.out.println("Here is the initial car details:");
System.out.println(initialCar);
System.out.println("Here are the cloned car details:");
System.out.println(clonedCar);
System.out.println("==============================");

System.out.println("Updating the initial car now.");
initialCar.updateCar("F-150", "Red", 50000);
System.out.println("\nOnce again,verifying the change effect...");
System.out.println("The initial car details:");
System.out.println(initialCar);
System.out.println("The cloned car details:");
System.out.println(clonedCar);
    }
}
```

Output

The program produces the following output:

```
***Prototype Pattern Demo***

The initial car details:
Company:Ford, Model: Maverick, Color:Silver, Price:25000.0
```

Getting another Ford car with some default settings by cloning.
The cloned car details:
Company:Ford, Model: Not defined, Color:Not set, Price:0.0

==============================
Updating the cloned car now.

Verifying the change effect on both cars...
Here is the initial car details:
Company:Ford, Model: Maverick, Color:Silver, Price:25000.0

Here are the cloned car details:
Company:Ford, Model: Ranger, Color:Blue, Price:40000.0

==============================
Updating the initial car now.

Once again,verifying the change effect...
The initial car details:
Company:Ford, Model: F-150, Color:Red, Price:50000.0

The cloned car details:
Company:Ford, Model: Ranger, Color:Blue, Price:40000.0

Analysis

Initially, I created a *Maverick* Ford car and set its price to $25,000. From this, I produced a cloned instance **using a deep copy**, ensuring that the Model object and other mutable fields were duplicated rather than shared. Notice that after the cloning process, the model was left undefined, the color was not set, and the price was reset to zero.

Next, I updated the cloned car by setting its model to *Ranger*, its color to blue, and its price to $40,000. **These changes did not affect the original *Maverick* car.**

Finally, I modified the original *Maverick* car by changing the model to *F-150*, its color to red, and its price to $50,000. **As expected, these updates did not impact the cloned car as well.**

These steps confirm that our Prototype pattern implementation behaves correctly, with the original and cloned instances remaining independent of each other.

Q&A Session

Q4.1 "However, the model was left undefined during the cloning process, the color was not set, and the price was reset to zero." Was there any specific thought behind this?

It is true that often, cloning means copying states as well. However, I wanted to use the prototype as a template, where each new clone should start fresh, before I create different models by cloning an existing car. This is why you saw those reset operations. I acknowledge that this can be tricky in certain scenarios, but overall, this design choice keeps the prototype flexible and reusable without mixing up data from previous customers.

Q4.2 Do you mean that we should not make an exact copy while cloning?

Not exactly. There are some typical cases where you may want an exact copy, including its state and values. This is useful if you need to preserve the current state of the object—for example, cloning a stage of the game or one of its characters.

Q4.3 Suppose, while cloning the cars in Demonstration 1, I do not want to reset the model details of the existing car. In other words, I'd like to copy its model information as well. How can I do that?

In this implementation, while cloning, if needed, you can copy the model details of an existing car without calling the reset operation (see the commented line in bold) as follows:

```java
@Override
public Car clone() throws CloneNotSupportedException {
 // First, making a shallow copy
 Car clonedCar = (Car) super.clone();
 // For a deep copy, manually instantiate all the reference type(s)
 // The following code will copy the existing model info as well.
 clonedCar.model = new Model(clonedCar.model.modelName, clonedCar.model.color);
 // However, I'd like to reset the model info along with the price
 //clonedCar.resetModelAndPrice();
 return clonedCar;
}
```

Q4.4 Does the Prototype pattern force me to prefer deep copy over shallow copy?

The classical GoF book says that a shallow copy is often sufficient. So, the clone() method in Java can often serve your needs. However, the classical GoF also says the following:

> *...cloning prototypes with complex structures usually requires a deep copy, because the clone and the original must be independent.* ***Therefore you must ensure that the clone's components are clones of the prototype's components.*** *Cloning forces you to decide what if anything will be shared.*

You have seen that while describing the clone()method, the Javadoc (see Object (Java SE 25 & JDK 25)[2]) also says the following:

By convention, the object returned by this method should be independent of this object (which is being cloned). To achieve this independence, it may be necessary to modify one or more fields of the object returned by super.clone before returning it.

Q4.5 The deep copy is expensive compared to the shallow copy. Isn't it?

True. However, while copying an object, there is no escape if you need to take care of all the references. Though shallow copy is faster and less expensive, it serves your needs if the original object has the primitive fields only. On the contrary, though deep copy is expensive and slow, it is useful if the original object contains many fields that have references to other objects.

Q4.6 Can you show me a program that elaborates on the difference between a shallow copy and a deep copy in Java?

Let's comment out the code that is not required for the shallow copy in the clone() method of the Car class as follows:

```
@Override
public Car clone() throws CloneNotSupportedException {
  // First, making a shallow copy
  Car clonedCar = (Car) super.clone();
  // For a deep copy, manually instantiate all the reference type(s)
  // The following code will copy the existing model info as well.
  // clonedCar.model = new Model(clonedCar.model.modelName,
  // clonedCar.model.color);
```

---

[2] https://docs.oracle.com/en/java/javase/25/docs/api/java.base/java/lang/Object.html#clone

```
// However, I'd like to reset the model info along with the price
// clonedCar.resetModelAndPrice();
return clonedCar;
}
```

Now, if you execute the program again, you'll see that **the edits in the cloned car changed the original car as well (and vice versa)**. I have highlighted the key changes in bold. Here is the sample output:

```
***Prototype Pattern Demo***

The initial car details:
Company:Ford, Model: Maverick, Color:Silver, Price:25000.0

Getting another Ford car with some default settings by cloning.
The cloned car details:
Company:Ford, Model: Maverick, Color:Silver, Price:25000.0


============================
Updating the cloned car now.

Verifying the change effect on both cars...
Here is the initial car details:
Company:Ford, Model: Ranger, Color:Blue, Price:25000.0

Here are the cloned car details:
Company:Ford, Model: Ranger, Color:Blue, Price:40000.0


============================
Updating the initial car now.

Once again,verifying the change effect...
The initial car details:
Company:Ford, Model: F-150, Color:Red, Price:50000.0

The cloned car details:
Company:Ford, Model: F-150, Color:Red, Price:40000.0
```

Why did this happen? Let's try to understand the mechanism with a simple diagram (see Figure 4-2). Suppose you have an object X1 and it has a reference to another object, Y1.

Figure 4-2. *X1 has a reference to Y1*

After a shallow copy of X1, a new object (say, X2) will be created that will also reference Y1 (see Figure 4-3).

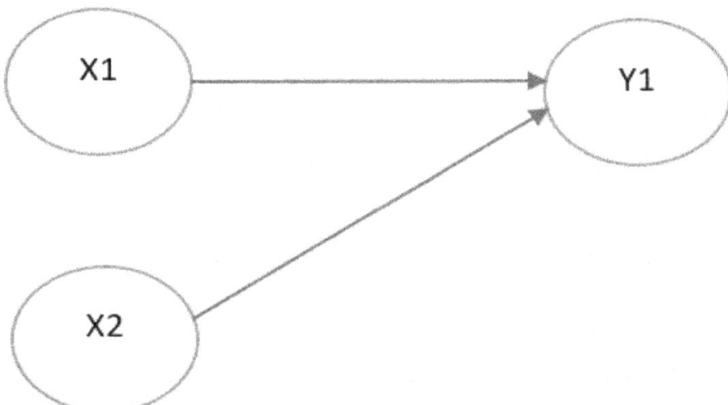

Figure 4-3. *After a shallow copy of X1, the new object X2 also references Y1*

On the contrary, after a deep copy of X1, a new object (say, X3) will be created, and X3 will have a reference to the new object Y3, which is a copy of Y1 (see Figure 4-4).

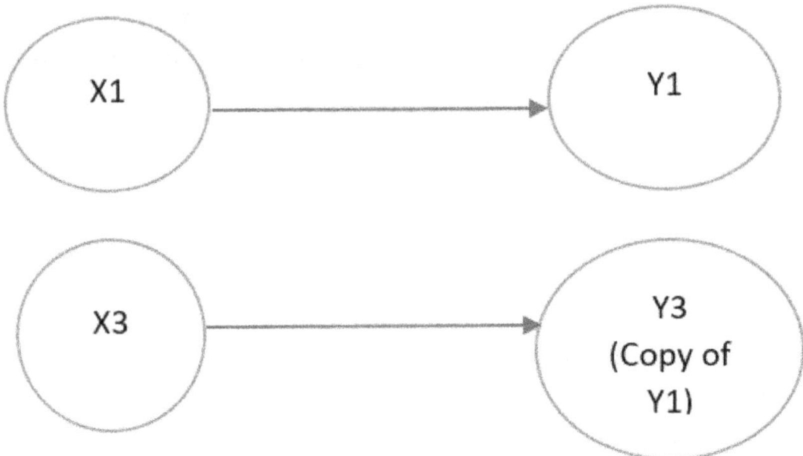

Figure 4-4. *After a deep copy of X1, the new object X3 references Y3, which is a copy of Y1*

Q4.7 A deep copy can be implemented in different ways. Isn't It?

Yes, that is correct. In this chapter, I used Java's built-in mechanism to implement the idea. You have seen that I have implemented the Cloneable interface and overridden the clone() method. However, there are several alternative approaches as well. Broadly, these fall into two categories:

- **Using copy constructors:** This approach gives you full control because the copying logic is explicitly written inside the constructor. The downside is that you must update the constructor whenever the class evolves.

POINT TO NOTE

If you would like to explore how the Prototype pattern can also be implemented using a **copy constructor**, refer to the prototype.demo1.alt package. It contains an alternative version of this demo that uses a copy constructor instead of the clone() method.

- **Using external libraries:** External libraries can offer excellent performance and support complex object graphs, but they come with the overhead of adding and maintaining third-party dependencies. For example, in Appendix A, you'll see one more approach where I used Apache Commons Lang's SerializationUtils.clone() to demonstrate deep copying and the Prototype pattern. This approach simplifies implementation but comes at the cost of performance and requires that all classes implement the Serializable interface.

Author's note: You can also use Kryo, which can perform automatic deep and shallow cloning. The details can be found at https://github.com/EsotericSoftware/kryo.

Alternative Implementation

Notice that in Demonstration 1, before cloning a car, the client created a Ford instance. It is OK. However, you may like to hide the instantiation process from the clients. In fact, the classical GoF book also promotes this idea by saying

> *When the number of prototypes in a system isn't fixed (that is, they can be created and destroyed dynamically), keep a registry of available prototypes. Clients won't manage prototypes themselves but will store and retrieve them from the registry. A client will ask the registry for a prototype before cloning it.*

To mimic the idea, let me show you an alternative implementation.

A Factory-Based Variation

In this version, I have made a few changes. Let us review them:

- I have introduced a new public class, called CarFactory, that stores the prototypes.

- I'll reuse the prototype.common package in this implementation. However, I created a separate package (**prototype.demo2**) for this demonstration and placed the CarFactory along with the Ford class in this package.

- **This time, the Ford class has the package-private visibility. So, the client cannot use it directly. As a result, the client needs to use the CarFactory class to get a Ford car.**

Let's see the CarFactory class now:

```java
// CarFactory.java
package prototype.demo2;

import prototype.common.Car;
import prototype.common.Model;
import java.util.Map;
import java.util.HashMap;

public class CarFactory {

  public static Map<String, Car> prototypes = new HashMap<>();
  static {
    // Will clone from a Maverick Ford car
    prototypes.put("ford", new Ford(new Model("Maverick", "Silver"), 25000));
    // Add other prototypes if any
  }
```

```
public static Car getPrototypeOf(String car) throws CloneNotSupportedException {
    Car getPrototype = prototypes.get(car);
    if (getPrototype == null) {
        throw new IllegalArgumentException("Unknown car type: " + car);
    }
    return getPrototype.clone();
  }
}
```

The following diagram (Figure 4-5) will help you visualize the design of the application.

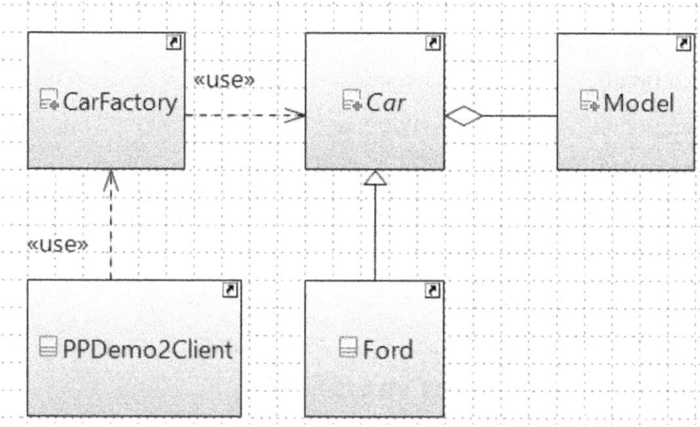

Figure 4-5. *The class diagram of the Prototype pattern implementation in Demonstration 2*

Demonstration 2

Here is a sample client code (PPDemo2Client.java) that uses this alternative implementation:

```
package prototype.demo2.client;
```

```java
import prototype.common.Car;
import prototype.demo2.CarFactory;

class PPDemo2Client {
  public static void main(String[] args) throws CloneNotSupportedException {
    System.out.println("***Prototype Pattern Demo-2***\n");
    System.out.println("Getting a Ford car with some default settings by cloning.");
    // Error now (Model class is not imported here)
    // Model model = new Model("Maverick", "Silver");
    // Error now even if you import the Model class
    // Car initialCar = new Ford(model, 25000);
    Car clonedCar = CarFactory.getPrototypeOf("ford");
    System.out.println(clonedCar);
    System.out.println("=============================");
    System.out.println("Updating the model and price of the cloned car now.");
    clonedCar.updateCar("Ranger", "Blue",40000);
    System.out.println("After update, here are the new car details:");
    System.out.println(clonedCar);
    System.out.println("=============================");
    System.out.println("Getting another Ford car with some default settings by cloning.");
    Car clonedCar2 = CarFactory.getPrototypeOf("ford");
    System.out.println(clonedCar2);
  }
}
```

Output

Here is the output:

```
***Prototype Pattern Demo-2***
```

Getting a Ford car with some default settings by cloning.
Company:Ford, Model: Not defined, Color:Not set, Price:0.0

```
==============================
```
Updating the model and price of the cloned car now.
After update, here are the new car details:
Company:Ford, Model: Ranger, Color:Blue, Price:40000.0

```
==============================
```
Getting another Ford car with some default settings by cloning.
Company:Ford, Model: Not defined, Color:Not set, Price:0.0

Q&A Session

Q4.8 What are the advantages of using the Prototype design pattern?

Here are some important usages:

- You can create new objects quickly without going through complex initialization steps.

- You can introduce minor variations without building a completely new object from scratch.

- You can include or discard products at runtime.

- You can focus on the key activities rather than on complicated instance creation processes.

- You can use a cloned object as a safe sandbox to preview and validate future behavior without affecting the original object.

Q4.9 What are the challenges associated with using the Prototype design pattern?

Here are some challenges:

- If shallow copy is not enough, you are forced to implement a deep copy mechanism. Implementing a deep copy is not always easy if you work with complex object graphs (e.g., objects that contain nested objects, collections, or circular references).

- In Demonstration 2, you used a registry of prototypes. However, maintaining this registry is an additional overhead because you must ensure that it stays in sync with actual objects.

- Earlier, I mentioned that deep copying can be implemented in different ways, and each approach has its own pros and cons (see Q4.7). For example, a serialization-based cloning (such as using SerializationUtils.clone()) can simplify an implementation, but it comes at the cost of performance and requires that all classes implement Serializable, which is always mandatory for serialization.

- In short, if the object construction is simple, or when classes don't lend themselves well to cloning (e.g., heavy reliance on external resources, circular references), you'd like to avoid the Prototype pattern.

Q4.10 How does the Prototype pattern differ from the Factory Method pattern?

The Factory Method promotes subclassing. In Chapter 1, you saw different factories produce different vehicles. For example, CarFactory produced cars, whereas the MotorcycleFactory produced motorcycles. These were specialized factories that formed a hierarchy of creator classes. **On the contrary, the Prototype pattern focuses on cloning to make a new object.** So, this pattern does not force you to form a creator class hierarchy. In short, the Factory Method emphasizes **creation through subclassing**, while the Prototype pattern emphasizes **creation through cloning objects**.

Q4.11 The CarFactory class used a static initialization block to store prototypes. Was this intentional?

Yes, it was intentional. The prototypes map is declared as a **static** Map<String, Car>, and the **static initialization block** populates this map when the class is first loaded. This ensures that all prototype objects are created only once and are available before any thread accesses the factory. Because class loading and static initialization are handled by the JVM in a thread-safe manner, this approach also simplifies usage in a multithreaded environment.

POINT TO NOTE

In Appendix A, you'll see one more approach where I used Apache Commons Lang's SerializationUtils.clone() to demonstrate deep copying and the Prototype pattern.

Summary

In this chapter, you explored two possible implementations of the Prototype design pattern, compared this pattern with the Factory Method Pattern, and analyzed the difference between a shallow copy and a deep copy. For now, you can move to the final chapter and continue learning another interesting pattern called Dependency Injection.

CHAPTER 5

Dependency Injection Pattern

Dependency Injection (DI) is a useful design pattern that helps achieve Inversion of Control (IoC) between classes and dependencies. This chapter discusses this pattern using various techniques.

WHAT IS INVERSION OF CONTROL?

In simple terms, a class does not create or manage its own dependencies. Instead, the control of creating and providing these dependencies is "inverted" to another class or framework, allowing the class to focus only on its core responsibilities.

Concept

Once you understand the need, the importance of this pattern becomes clear. Let's first look at a program that produces the expected result but is difficult to maintain.

© Vaskaran Sarcar 2026
V. Sarcar, *Creational Design Patterns in Java*, Apress Pocket Guides,
https://doi.org/10.1007/979-8-8688-2314-5_5

A Sample Program

Throughout the book, we made lots of cars. Let us work with them one more time. This time, the Car is a simple class:

```java
// Car.java
package di.demo1;

public class Car {
  private final String type;
  public Car() {
    this.type = "car";
  }
  public String travel(int speed) {
    String msg = this + " at " + speed + " mph";
    return msg;
  }
  @Override
  public String toString() {
    return type;
  }
}
```

Author's note: Although the travel() method does not directly access the type instance variable, it still uses it indirectly. When the method prints this, Java automatically calls toString(), which returns the value stored in type. This ensures that the car's type appears in the output message.

Let's create another class (Driver) that'd like to drive the cars (i.e., the Car instances):

```java
// Driver.java
package di.demo1;

public class Driver {
```

```
  private Car car;
  public Driver() {
    car = new Car();
  }
  public void drive(int speed) {
    System.out.println("The driver can drive a " + car.travel(speed));
  }
}
```

To make things easy, before you see the client code (DIDemo1Client.java), let us visualize the class diagram (Figure 5-1).

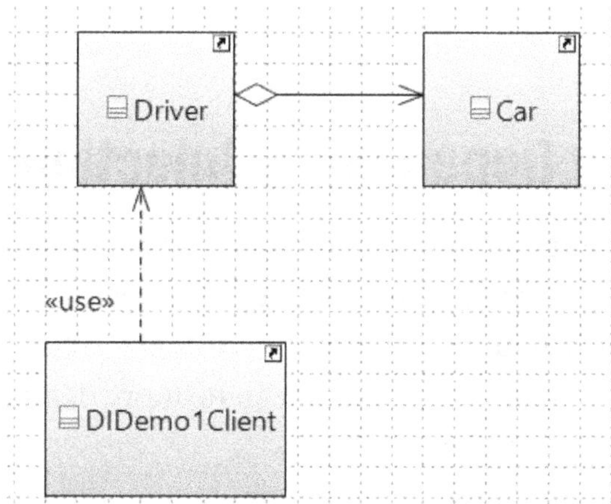

Figure 5-1. *In Demonstration 1, the Driver class directly creates and depends on the Car class*

Demonstration 1

Let me show you a sample client code:

// DIDemo1Client.java

```
package di.demo1.client;

import di.demo1.Driver;
```

```
class DIDemo1Client {
    public static void main(String[] args) {
        Driver driver = new Driver();
        driver.drive(100);
    }
}
```

Output

There is no surprise that when you execute this program, you'll see the following output:

The driver can drive a car at 100 mph

Introducing Dependency Injection

The Driver class created a Car instance inside its constructor in the previous program. **It's like you book a car and the driver brings a car for you. In this case, the driver depends on the car while travelling and gets your payment.** However, real-life situations can be more demanding. Let's look at some real-world scenarios as follows.

Real-Life Example

In Demonstration 1, maintaining the car is the driver's responsibility. However, it is possible that you may not like the driver's car. Instead, you'd like to travel with your car and hire a driver (let's assume that you do not want to drive). In this case, the driver can fully focus on his job (i.e., driving), and his payment is no longer dependent on the car. In other words, the driver does not worry about the car's maintenance anymore. This example shows that the driver's dependency on the car is reduced.

> **POINT TO NOTE**
>
> In Demonstration 1, a Car object was created inside the Driver class's constructor. This code segment reflects that the Driver class was tightly coupled with the Car class. DI primarily targets to reduce the coupling between classes to make them easily reusable, testable, and maintainable. As a result, the concurrent development becomes easy as well. To make the discussion easy, I made this class simple.

Finding other real-life examples is easy as well. For example, when I worked for my employer, I did not need to worry about the servicing of the laptop. However, for my personal laptop, I may need to go to a laptop service shop if it starts malfunctioning or requires any improvements. You can see that my dependency on a laptop varies according to the situation.

Computer World Example

Jakarta EE is the modern successor to Java EE. The online Jakarta EE Tutorial[1] states the following:

> *Dependency injection enables you to turn regular Java classes into managed objects and to inject them into any other managed object. Using dependency injection, your code can declare dependencies on any managed object. The container automatically provides instances of these dependencies at the injection points at runtime, and it also manages the lifecycle of these instances for you.*

---

[1] https://jakartaee.github.io/jakartaee-documentation/jakartaee-tutorial/current/platform/injection/injection.html

Microsoft (see Dependency injection - .NET | Microsoft Learn[2]) also states the following:

> *.NET supports the dependency injection (DI) software design pattern, which is a technique for achieving Inversion of Control (IoC) between classes and their dependencies. Dependency injection in .NET is a built-in part of the framework, along with configuration, logging, and the options pattern.*

You can see that DI is common in the programming world.

POINT TO NOTE

This chapter gives you the core idea of DI. So, it is no wonder that you can implement these ideas in a different programming language (such as C#) as well.

Types of DI

While applying DI, you'd like to avoid the situation where a class creates its own dependencies. Instead, you'd like to use an external entity (often termed as an **injector**) that will provide those dependencies. This is why, while improving Demonstration 1, you'd not allow the Driver class to create its own dependencies (the Car class in our example).

Now the question is: How to implement the idea? You can implement it in various ways, such as

- Constructor injection

- Setter injection (often called Property injection)

---

[2] https://learn.microsoft.com/en-us/dotnet/core/extensions/dependency-injection

- Method injection

- Interface injection

Let's start the discussion with the constructor injection (CI).

Constructor Injection

In this section, you'll see two programs. In the first program, I'll show you a simple technique to overcome the tight coupling between the Driver class and the Car class. In the next program, I'll enhance the capability of the program.

Demonstration 2

Here, I present a new version of the Driver class:

```
package di.demo2;

public class Driver {
  private Car car;
  public Driver(Car car) {
    this.car = car; // Injecting the car
  }
  public void drive(int speed) {
    System.out.println("The driver can drive a " + car.travel(speed));
  }
}
```

Author's note: There is no change in the Car class. This class is now placed in the same package (di.demo2)—so that the Driver class can access it. Remember that all classes within each demonstration in this chapter reside in the same package.

Notice that in Demonstration 2, the Driver class continues to depend on the Car type, but it no longer constructs a Car object. The creation responsibility is moved outside the Driver class. **This separation of concerns loosens the coupling because the Driver now uses a Car that is supplied to it, rather than deciding which Car to create.**

More specifically, a client of the Driver class will now be responsible for supplying this Car instance. **In the upcoming demonstration, the DIDemo2Client.java is the client that plays the role of "creator" or "injector" of dependencies.** To make things easy, before you see the client code (DIDemo2Client.java), let us visualize the class diagram (Figure 5-2).

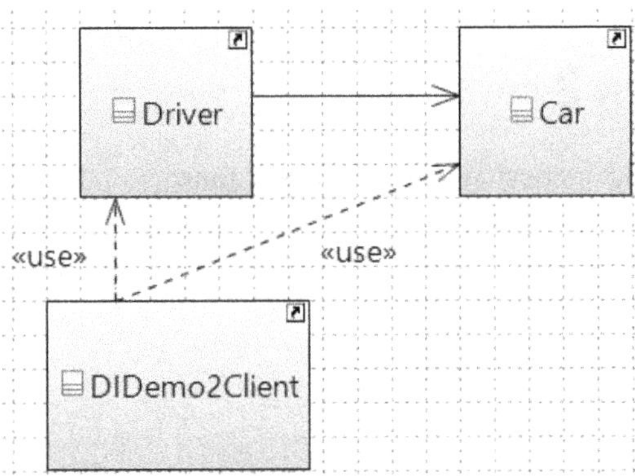

Figure 5-2. *In Demonstration 2, the driver no longer "owns" the car*

Here is a sample client code:

```java
// DIDemo2Client.java
package di.demo2.client;

import di.demo2.Car;
import di.demo2.Driver;

class DIDemo2Client {
    public static void main(String[] args) {
        Car car = new Car();
```

```
    Driver driver = new Driver(car);
    driver.drive(100);
  }
}
```

Output

Upon executing this program, you'll see the same output:

The driver can drive a car at 100 mph

Q&A Session

Q5.1 Why do you think that Demonstration 2 is an improvement over Demonstration 1?

In Demonstration 2, the Driver class is no longer tied to the specific Car implementation. It means that you have **loosened the coupling** between the Driver class and the Car class. Here, the responsibility of creating a car is separate from the responsibility of using it. The client (DIDemo2Client) now manages the creation and wiring of objects, while the Driver class can focus solely on driving. It means that Demonstration 2 also focused on the **separation of concerns**.

DEMONSTRATION 1 VS. DEMONSTRATION 2

In essence, in Demonstration 1, the driver said, "**I need to create a car before I drive.**" On the contrary, in Demonstration 2, the driver said, "**If someone provides me with a car, I'm ready to drive.**" This shift is the fundamental principle of Dependency Injection.

Enhancing the Program

Let's assume that the driver is a smart guy who can also drive a different type of vehicle, such as a bus. How can you accommodate these capabilities in this program? You guessed it right! You can introduce an interface and inherit the concrete classes from it.

Author's note: In this demonstration, Vehicle is defined as an interface to keep the example simple and focused on dependency injection. An abstract class could also be used if we needed shared state or base implementations, but that is not required in this minimal design.

POINT TO NOTE

Since I'll reuse this vehicle hierarchy in the upcoming examples, I created a separate package (di.vehicles) to maintain different vehicles. For the remainder of this chapter, you can safely assume that this vehicle hierarchy is in place; I'll only show the changes to the Driver and client classes.

Here is the interface, called Vehicle:

```java
// Vehicle.java
package di.vehicles;

public interface Vehicle {
    String travel(int speed);
}
```

Now the Car class can inherit from it:

```java
// Car.java

public class Car implements Vehicle {
    private final String type;
```

```java
  public Car() {
    this.type = "car";
  }
  @Override
  public String travel(int speed) {
    String msg = this + " at " + speed + " mph";
    return msg;
  }
  @Override
  public String toString() {
    return type;
  }
}
```

The Bus class is very similar to the Car class. Let's see it now:

// Bus.java

```java
package di.vehicles;

public class Bus implements Vehicle {
  private final String type;
  public Bus() {
    this.type= "bus";
  }
  @Override
  public String travel(int speed) {
    String msg = this + " at " + speed + " mph";
    return msg;
  }
  @Override
  public String toString() {
    return type;
  }
}
```

It's time to adjust the changes in the Driver class as well (notice the key changes in bold):

```java
// Driver.java
package di.demo3;

import di.vehicles.Vehicle;

public class Driver {
    private Vehicle vehicle;
    public Driver(Vehicle vehicle) {
        this.vehicle = vehicle;
    }
    public void drive(int speed) {
        System.out.println("The driver can drive a " + vehicle.travel(speed));
    }
}
```

To make things easy, before you see the client code (DIDemo3Client.java), let us visualize the relationship among the classes in the following class diagram (Figure 5-3).

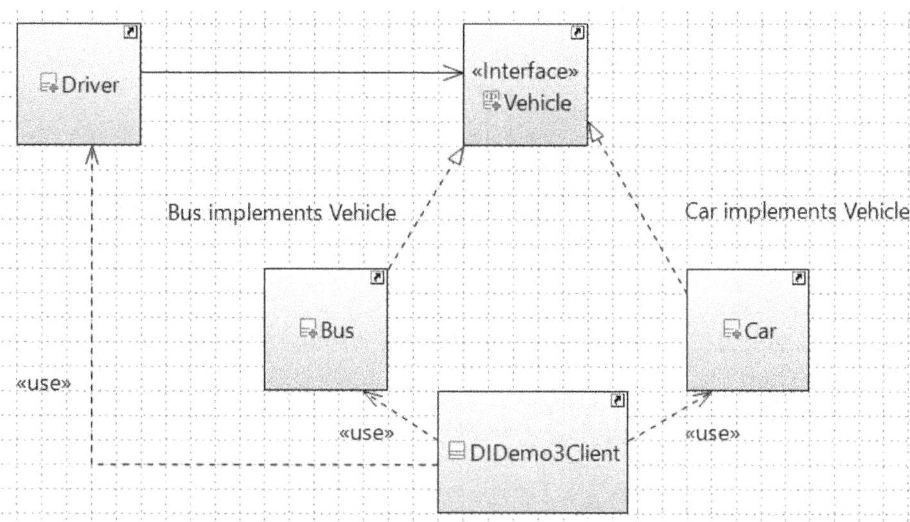

Figure 5-3. *The Driver class now knows about the Vehicle type, but not a concrete implementation (such as Car or Bus) of it*

Demonstration 3

Now, see the client code:

// DIDemo3Client.java

```java
package di.demo3.client;

import di.vehicles.*;
import di.demo3.Driver;

class DIDemo3Client {
    public static void main(String[] args) {
        Vehicle vehicle = new Car();
        Driver driver = new Driver(vehicle);
        driver.drive(100);
```

```
    vehicle = new Bus();
    driver = new Driver(vehicle);
    driver.drive(150);
    }
}
```

Output

Once you execute this program, you'll see the following output:

```
The driver can drive a car at 100 mph
The driver can drive a bus at 150 mph
```

Q&A Session

Q5.2 How does Demonstration 3 differ from Demonstration 2?

Though Demonstration 2 successfully used Dependency Injection, the Driver was still coupled to the Car class. In that code, if you want the driver to drive a new vehicle, say a bus, you need to change the Driver's constructor and field type.

Demonstration 3 solves this by depending on an abstraction (Vehicle interface) rather than a concrete implementation (Car class). **This use of polymorphism allows the Driver class to work with any type of vehicle.**

Since the Driver class is decoupled from the specific type of vehicle it is driving, using the power of polymorphism, you can anytime introduce a new type of vehicle (e.g., the Truck class) that implements the Vehicle interface. However, you do not need to modify the Driver class at all, as long as it receives a Vehicle object in its constructor. This makes the system easily extendable as well as maintainable. In fact, Demonstration 3 promotes the idea of the **Dependency Inversion Principle (DIP)**, which is the "D" in SOLID principles (briefly discussed in Chapter 1).

Author's note: The DIP principle states that high-level modules (like Driver) should not depend on low-level modules (e.g., Car or Bus), but rather on abstractions (e.g., Vehicle).

Q5.3 Does Demonstration 3 fully follow the DIP principle?

Notice that the Driver class (**the high-level module**) depends on the Vehicle abstraction. This part follows DIP.

The Car and Bus classes (**low-level modules**) depend on the Vehicle abstraction (by implementing it) as well. This part also follows DIP.

However, for the "**Inversion**," the client (DIDemo3Client) should not directly create the low-level objects. Instead, it could ask a factory or a container for the Vehicle it needs. So, you can say that Demonstration 3 partially violates the DIP principle.

Q5.4 Does the constructor injection force me to use an interface instead of a concrete class?

No. However, in Demonstration 3, I used multiple vehicles. This was the primary reason for using the interface Vehicle.

You may also remember that one of the key design principles in OOP is to program to an interface, but not an implementation. So, it's a good practice to focus on the Vehicle interface, instead of concrete classes such as Car (or Bus) that implement Vehicle.

However, these do not force you to consider constructor injection using an interface type. Demonstration 2 showed you an example without using an interface. **What is mandatory in constructor injection is that the dependency must be supplied from outside—the class itself must not create it internally.**

Setter Injection

You can also have setter injection (sometimes called property injection in other ecosystems such as .NET). To demonstrate this, let us introduce a setter in the Driver class. Here is the new look of the Driver class (notice that this time, you do not define any constructor):

```java
// Driver.java
package di.demo4;

import di.vehicles.Vehicle;

 public class Driver {
   private Vehicle vehicle;
   public void setVehicle(Vehicle vehicle) {
     this.vehicle = vehicle;
   }
   public void drive(int speed) {
     System.out.println("The driver can drive a " + vehicle.travel(speed));
   }
}
```

Except for the client code (DIDemo4Client.java), you do not need to make any other changes for the following demonstration.

Demonstration 4

Let's see how a client can handle the change now.

```java
// DIDemo4Client.java

package di.demo4.client;

import di.vehicles.*;
import di.demo4.Driver;
```

```java
class DIDemo4Client {
  public static void main(String[] args) {

    Vehicle vehicle = new Car();
    Driver driver = new Driver();
    driver.setVehicle(vehicle);
    driver.drive(100);

    // Creating a new vehicle
    vehicle = new Bus();
    // Letting the driver drive the new vehicle
    driver.setVehicle(vehicle);
    driver.drive(150);
  }
}
```

Output

There is no surprise that you'll get the following output:

```
The driver can drive a car at 100 mph
The driver can drive a bus at 150 mph
```

Analysis

Notice the client code again. This time, you allow the **same** driver to drive a new vehicle (bus). This means that, unlike constructor injection, this allows you to inject a new dependency (Bus) into the **same Driver instance** without having to create a new Driver object. This runtime flexibility is the main advantage of Setter Injection. On the contrary, if you do not set the vehicle before driving the car, you'll encounter a NullPointerException.

Q&A Session

Q5.5 "If you do not set the vehicle before driving the car, you'll encounter a NullPointerException." Can you please elaborate?

If the vehicle field inside the Driver object is null, invoking the drive method on a Driver instance (driver) can cause this exception. To verify this, let's comment out the following line (shown in bold) in the client code:

```
// There is no change in the package and import statements
class DIDemo4Client {
  public static void main(String[] args) {

    Vehicle vehicle = new Car();
    Driver driver = new Driver();
    //driver.setVehicle(vehicle);
    driver.drive(100);
    // The remaining code is not shown
```

And execute the program again. This time, you'll see the NullPointerException. Here is a sample output:

Exception in thread "main" java.lang.NullPointerException: **Cannot invoke "di.vehicles.Vehicle.travel(int)" because "this.vehicle" is null**
        at di.demo4.Driver.drive(Driver.java:16)
        at di.demo4.DIDemo4Client.main(DIDemo4Client.java:13)

Q5.6 Can we combine different injection techniques?

Yes, you can (in fact, you'd like to do this to make your application better). For example, while creating a Driver instance, you could inject a vehicle using constructor injection (following Demonstration 3). Later, you could set a new vehicle for the same Driver instance (following Demonstration 4).

Method Injection

The constructor injection (CI) allows you to pass dependencies as arguments to the constructors. You can do the same to a specific method as well. Let me show you an example by updating the previous program.

Here is the new look of the Driver class:

```java
package di.demo5;

import di.vehicles.Vehicle;

public class Driver {
    public void drive(Vehicle vehicle, int speed) {
        System.out.println("The driver can drive a " + vehicle.travel(speed));
    }
}
```

Author's note: Notice that the Driver class in this demonstration does not maintain a Vehicle instance variable. Instead, the drive() method accepts the vehicle along with the speed as method parameters. This is another way to supply the required dependency.

Except for the client code (DIDemo5Client.java), you do not need any other changes for the following demonstration.

Demonstration 5

Let's see how a client can handle the change:

```java
// DIDemo5Client.java

package di.demo5.client;

import di.vehicles.*;
import di.demo5.Driver;
```

```
class DIDemo5Client {
  public static void main(String[] args) {
    Vehicle vehicle = new Car();
    Driver driver = new Driver();
    driver.drive(vehicle, 100);

    // Creating a new vehicle
    vehicle = new Bus();
    // Letting the driver drive the new vehicle
    driver.drive(vehicle, 150);
  }
}
```

Output

Once again, the same driver could drive both a car and a bus. Here is the output:

```
The driver can drive a car at 100 mph
The driver can drive a bus at 150 mph
```

Q&A Session

Q5.7 When should I prefer method injections?

The method injections are useful to inject the temporary dependencies. They can also serve you when you have different implementations for various method calls.

Q5.8 "They can also serve you when you have different implementations for various method calls." Can you please elaborate?

Method injection promotes a powerful form of polymorphism and decoupling. To illustrate, notice the drive method in the Driver class once again:

```
public void drive(Vehicle vehicle, int speed) {
    System.out.println("The driver can drive a " + vehicle.travel(speed));
}
```

Since the Car class implements the Vehicle interface, you can pass a Car object to this method and, eventually, invoke the travel method defined in the Car class. Similarly, by passing a Bus object to the drive method, you can invoke the travel method defined in the Bus class. **The drive method does not care how this method is implemented in the Car class or the Bus class; it only cares whether the object passed to it can invoke the travel method.** This makes the code flexible, reusable, and testable.

Q5.9 How does it make the testing easy?

You can pass a mock (or fake) object that does not drive a regular vehicle, such as a car or a bus.

Interface Injection

I'll now discuss the **interface injection** technique. Its overall architecture is a little bit complex compared to the previous DI techniques. However, it adds more flexibility and extendibility in your application. **To make things easy, I'll enhance Demonstration 4 with some minor changes to illustrate the technique.** Let's explore this.

In Demonstration 4, you saw **setter injection**, where the dependent class (Driver) provided a public setter method, and the client code directly supplied the dependency. Though useful, this setter injection lacks a formal contract and doesn't enforce consistency across multiple clients.

Now, the dependent class implements a dedicated **injection interface** (VehicleUser) that defines a method for receiving its dependency. This allows a separate injector (VehicleInjector) to supply dependencies without knowing the details of each concrete client class (such as Driver).

Author's note: In Dependency Injection literature, the word client usually means the class that depends on an abstraction (e.g., Driver or Mechanic that depends on Vehicle). However, in everyday programming, we often call the class with public static void main (e.g., DIDemo6Client) the client program or driver class, because it uses the whole setup. So, in the previous paragraph, I mentioned it explicitly.

How does it help? Until now, drivers have used the vehicles. However, there are other categories of people who can use these vehicles. For example, if a vehicle does not provide a satisfactory service, a driver can take it to a service center where a mechanic can fix the issue. In this scenario, the driver and the mechanic both work on the same vehicle. The upcoming design can easily accommodate this scenario.

POINT TO NOTE

The upcoming program (Demonstration 6) demonstrates a minimal yet complete example of interface injection. The key point is that the injection contract is **defined by the interface**, ensuring consistency and enabling flexibility, even when the system grows to include multiple client types.

Ok, let us start with the following interface:

```java
// VehicleUser.java
package di.demo6.users;

import di.vehicles.Vehicle;

// The injectable interface
public interface VehicleUser {
   void  setVehicle(Vehicle vehicle);
}
```

Now, the Driver class can implement the interface as follows:

// Driver.java

```java
package di.demo6.users;

import di.vehicles.Vehicle;

 public class Driver implements VehicleUser {
   private Vehicle vehicle;
   @Override
   public void setVehicle(Vehicle vehicle) {
    this.vehicle = vehicle;
   }
   public void drive(int speed) {
    System.out.println("The driver can drive a " + vehicle.travel(speed));
   }
 }
```

POINT TO NOTE

You can see that I have stored the VehicleUser and Driver together in a separate package (di.users) to maintain different users of the vehicles. For the same reason, I needed to enhance the corresponding visibility (I made them public).

In the same package, you will later see a Mechanic class that also implements VehicleUser. I will discuss that example in Q5.13.

Now see the injector:

```java
package di.demo6.injector;

import di.demo6.users.VehicleUser;
import di.vehicles.Bus;
```

```java
import di.vehicles.Car;

public class VehicleInjector {

    private VehicleInjector() { }

    public static void configureWithCar(VehicleUser user) {
        user.setVehicle(new Car());
    }

    public static void configureWithBus(VehicleUser user) {
        user.setVehicle(new Bus());
    }
}
```

Since the architecture is relatively complex, let me show you the class diagram as well (see Figure 5-4).

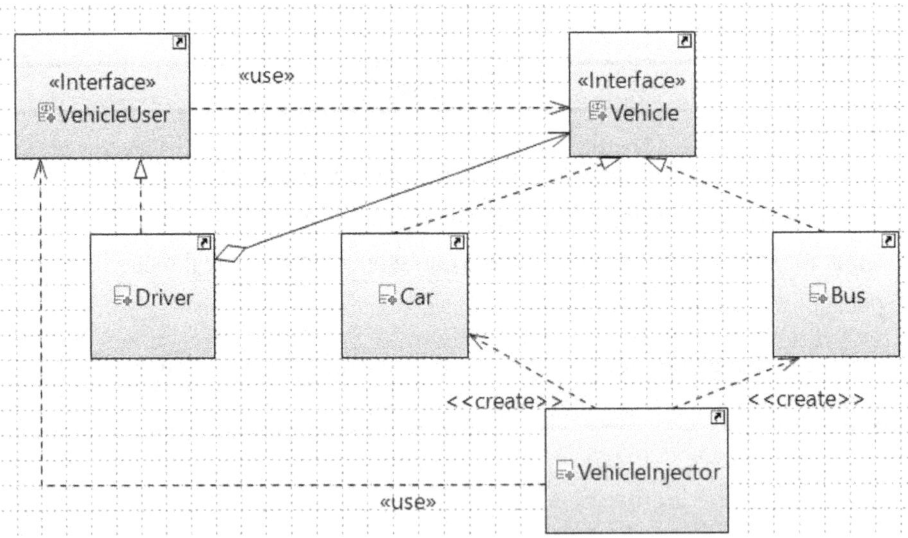

Figure 5-4. *The class diagram after the interface injection. The Driver class depends on the Vehicle abstraction, and a separate VehicleInjector is responsible for setting the dependency*

Demonstration 6

Let's see how a client can handle these changes:

// DIDemo6Client.java

```java
package di.demo6.client;

import di.demo6.users.*;
import di.demo6.injector.VehicleInjector;

class DIDemo6Client {
  public static void main(String[] args) {
    Driver driver = new Driver();
    // Let the driver drive a car
    VehicleInjector.configureWithCar(driver);
    driver.drive(100);
    // Let the driver drive a bus
    VehicleInjector.configureWithBus(driver);
    driver.drive(150);
  }
}
```

Output

There is no surprise that you'll get the following output:

```
The driver can drive a car at 100 mph
The driver can drive a bus at 150 mph
```

POINT TO NOTE

In a strict, academic sense, a pure interface injection framework would completely determine the dependency internally; the client would provide the dependent object (e.g., a Driver instance) and would *not* indicate which specific implementation it needs. The injector would examine its configuration files, annotations, or metadata, and then, based on those rules, it would decide whether the client should receive a Car, a Bus, or any other concrete Vehicle. The key idea is that the choice of dependency is made entirely by the injector, not by the client, which ensures full decoupling between object creation and object usage.

However, in this demonstration, the client calls configureWithCar() or configureWithBus() to indicate the dependency. I deliberately made this choice for clarity and to make things easy for you. It keeps the example transparent, demonstrates Inversion of Control, and shows how the dependent object (Driver) receives its dependency via an interface, without the added complexity of a full DI container.

Q&A Session

Q5.10 Why is Demonstration 6 an example of interface injection but not simply a setter injection?

It is true that at first glance, Demonstration 6 might look like setter injection because it uses a method named setVehicle. However, there is a crucial difference. Let's analyze:

In Demonstration 4 (setter injection), the dependent class (Driver) just provides a public setter method. The client code (DIDemo4Client) itself acts as the injector by directly calling this setter. However, notice that there is no explicit contract that forces classes to expose such a method—it is only by convention.

Now analyze Demonstration 6 (interface injection). Here, the injection method (setVehicle) is not just an ordinary setter; it is part of the VehicleUser interface. So, any class (such as Driver or Mechanic) that wants to receive a Vehicle must implement this interface. In this implementation, a dedicated injector class (VehicleInjector) performs the injection, and it only needs to work with the VehicleUser interface, not with each concrete class.

In short, Demonstration 6 is interface injection because the injection contract is defined and enforced by an interface (VehicleUser). This makes injection consistent and explicit across multiple classes. In contrast, Demonstration 4 is setter injection because the injection point is just a plain setter method defined directly in the dependent class, with no formal interface contract.

At the end, I also want you to note that a setter injection and an interface injection are not mutually exclusive. In fact, our Demonstration 6 can be thought of as an interface-based setter injection as well.

Q5.11 Can you summarize the differences between the different dependency injection techniques?

In the case of constructor injections, **you provide all the dependencies at the time of instantiation (it is mandatory). You cannot change these dependencies after the instantiation process (the dependency becomes effectively immutable).**

In the case of setter DI or method DI, **you can alter the dependencies after the object is created.** For example, in the corresponding demonstrations (Demonstration 4 and Demonstration 5), you saw the instantiation of the Driver class only once. Still, you have seen that the same driver was able to drive both a car and a bus. However, you need to be careful. It is because **if the dependencies are not set properly, you'll encounter unwanted outcomes. On the contrary, the constructor injection ensures that a target class cannot be instantiated without the necessary dependencies.**

The interface injection is **comparatively complex compared to others. However, it provides more flexibility**. Let me now show a quick comparison using the following table (see Table 5-1).

Table 5-1. *Comparison of Dependency Injection Techniques*

DI Type	How to Apply?	Flexibility	Key Points
Constructor Injection	Via constructor	Fixed at creation	Object cannot exist without dependencies. Dependencies cannot be changed after creations
Setter Injection	Via setter method	Changeable at runtime	Can replace dependency after an object creation. However, if the dependencies are not set properly, you can see the NullPointerException
Method Injection	As method parameter	Temporary/per call	Useful for varying dependencies per call
Interface Injection	Implements injector interface	Changeable at runtime	Enforces the contract and is easily extendable. However, the overall architecture is complex compared to other techniques

You can see that each approach has its own pros and cons. So, choose the approach that can improve your application. As said before, you can also combine multiple approaches if needed.

Q5.12 Earlier, you briefly talked about the Dependency Inversion. I would like to hear more on that. It'll also be helpful if you discuss how it differs from Dependency Injection.

Dependency Injection (DI) is a design pattern/technique that you learned in this chapter. Dependency Inversion is a design principle (often termed as DIP) that promotes loose coupling and abstraction. *DIP can be achieved through DI.*

I have discussed DIP in detail in my other book, *Simple and Efficient Programming in C# Second Edition* (Apress, 2022).[3] For now, let me pick some portions from that book to give you a basic idea.

DIP tells two important things:

- A high-level concrete class should not depend on a low-level concrete class. Instead, both should depend on abstractions.

- Abstractions should not depend upon details. Instead, the details should depend upon abstractions.

POINT TO NOTE

In his book, *Agile Principles, Patterns, and Practices in C#* (Pearson, First Edition, 2006),[4] Robert C. Martin explains that in traditional procedural programming, high-level modules often end up depending on low-level modules. Object-oriented programming, however, aims to reverse this dependency structure. In OOP, both high-level and low-level modules should depend on abstractions, which prevents high-level policies from being vulnerable to changes in low-level details. This inversion of dependencies is the key reason behind the term **Dependency Inversion Principle**.

---

[3] https://link.springer.com/book/10.1007/978-1-4842-8737-8

[4] https://www.amazon.com/Principles-Patterns-Practices-Robert-Martin/dp/0131857258

Now, compare Figures 5-1 and 5-3 again. In Figure 5-1, the Driver class (the high-level concrete class) depended on the Car class (the low-level concrete class). However, after the constructor injection, in Figure 5-3, the Driver class and the Car class were both dependent on Vehicle. This structure fulfills the criteria for the DIP. How? Notice that this time, the Driver class targets the abstraction Vehicle, instead of a concrete implementation (Car). This gave you the flexibility to consider a new vehicle type (Bus) without altering the existing classes.

If you dive deep into the DIP, you'll understand the essence of the second part of the DIP as well. It is important because if an interface needs to change to support one of its clients, other clients can be impacted due to the change.

Author's note: Even with Java 8 default methods, care must be taken: changing an existing method in an interface can still impact other clients, so the second part of the DIP remains important.

In short, **DIP can be achieved through DI**. However, while working on DI, you'll often hear that it is used to achieve **Inversion of Control (IoC)**, which is a broader principle. Using the concept of IoC, you can pass the control of object creation and management from the dependent class or the application code to an external framework or container. In practice, well-known frameworks such as the Spring Framework rely heavily on IoC and Dependency Injection to wire objects, manage their lifecycles, and configure applications.[5] **A detailed discussion on IoC, DIP, or Spring is beyond the scope of this book.**

Author's note: Manually implementing dependency injections across a large code base is a challenging task. In that case, you can take help from a framework that supports this concept. In the Java ecosystem, the Spring Framework is widely adopted and is one of the most influential IoC

---

[5] https://docs.spring.io/spring-framework/docs/4.1.x/spring-framework-reference/html/beans.html

and Dependency Injection solutions. Need some other examples? If you come from a non-Java background, particularly .NET, you may find this community discussion useful to understand how Dependency Injection is viewed in that ecosystem: https://stackoverflow.com/questions/21288/which-net-dependency-injection-frameworks-are-worth-looking-into.

Q5.13 You said that interface injection adds flexibility and extendibility in my application. I'd like you to give an example.

Let's introduce a Mechanic class that implements VehicleUser. As a result, the Mechanic class must follow the contract that is defined in the VehicleUser interface. In other words, it needs to implement the setVehicle method. Here is a sample implementation:

```java
package di.demo6.users;

import di.vehicles.Vehicle;

public class Mechanic implements VehicleUser {
    private Vehicle vehicle;
    @Override
    public void setVehicle(Vehicle vehicle) {
        this.vehicle = vehicle;
    }
    public void drive(int speed) {
        System.out.println("After repairing, the mechanic can drive a " +
            vehicle.travel(speed));
    }
}
```

You can now use it in DIDemo6Client as follows (notice the changes in bold):

```java
package di.demo6;

import di.demo6.users.*;
import di.demo6.injector.VehicleInjector;
import di.vehicles.*;

class DIDemo6Client {

   public static void main(String[] args) {
      Driver driver = new Driver();
      // Let the driver drive a car
      VehicleInjector.configureWithCar(driver);
      driver.drive(100);

      // Let the driver drive a bus
      VehicleInjector.configureWithBus(driver);
      driver.drive(150);

      System.out.println("====================");

      Mechanic mechanic = new Mechanic();
      // Let the mechanic drive a car
      VehicleInjector.configureWithCar(mechanic);
      mechanic.drive(200);

      // Let the mechanic drive a bus
      VehicleInjector.configureWithBus(mechanic);
      mechanic.drive(250);

   }
}
```

Upon executing the modified program, you'll see the following output:

The driver can drive a car at 100 mph

The driver can drive a bus at 150 mph

====================

After repairing, the mechanic can drive a car at 200 mph

After repairing, the mechanic can drive a bus at 250 mph

Q5.14 Do you consider DI as a Creational design pattern?

At first look, DI may not appear as a creational pattern as per the definition of the classic GoF book. Still, it is often associated with creational patterns because it can influence how you create (and manage) objects in a system. In fact, if you see the interview with Erich Gamma, Richard Helm, and Ralph Johnson—"Design Patterns 15 Years Later: An Interview with Erich Gamma, Richard Helm, and Ralph Johnson," InformIT—or Ralph Johnson's talk at JDD2015 – Twenty-one Years of Design Patterns (Ralph Johnson), YouTube, you will see that DI is considered as a creational design pattern.

However, at the beginning of this chapter, you saw that Microsoft (see https://learn.microsoft.com/en-us/dotnet/core/extensions/dependency-injection/overview) considers DI as a technique for achieving Inversion of Control (IoC). Since IoC is an architectural pattern (see https://en.wikipedia.org/wiki/Design_Patterns), you can say that DI falls under the broader category of Architectural Patterns.

Interestingly, Wikipedia (see the same link) tagged Dependency Injection and Method Chaining in "Other Patterns." I already used method chaining while implementing the Builder pattern (see Demonstration 2 of Chapter 3). In the same way, you can use DI with other patterns to make a nice application. So, according to me, understanding the pattern is more important than tagging it with a category. If you still force me to pick only one general category for DI, I'd like to tag it as an Architectural pattern.

Summary

This chapter presented six demonstrations. Demonstration 1 explained the need for DI. Demonstrations 2 and 3 focused on constructor injection, demonstrating two ways to supply dependencies. Demonstration 4 covered setter injection, Demonstration 5 covered method injection, and Demonstration 6 illustrated interface injection. Table 5-1 compares the four injection techniques (constructor, setter, method, and interface injection). You saw how DI reduces coupling, improves flexibility, and makes code easier to maintain and test. From constructor injection to interface injection, each technique offers unique advantages, such as runtime flexibility, per-call dependency injection, or enforcing formal contracts.

Congratulations! You have now completed all the patterns in this book. You can apply these ideas to your projects, and I believe you will find them useful even when working in different programming languages. I hope you appreciate the effort and enjoy putting these patterns into practice. Happy coding!

Exploring Pattern Enhancements

Let's see how we can extend (or modify) some of the implementations in this book.

Revisiting Factory Pattern

You have learned the Factory Method pattern in Chapter 1. Let's explore it with more details now.

Parameterized Factory

In Demonstration 3 of Chapter 1, the CarFactory created cars, and the MotorcycleFactory created motorcycles. At the end of the chapter, I told you that using a parameterized factory, you can extend the idea where the CarFactory can produce different types of cars (e.g., regular cars and sports cars) and the MotorcycleFactory can produce different types of motorcycles (e.g., regular motorcycles and sports motorcycles). Let's see a sample implementation.

© Vaskaran Sarcar 2026
V. Sarcar, *Creational Design Patterns in Java*, Apress Pocket Guides,
https://doi.org/10.1007/979-8-8688-2314-5

Demonstration 1

First, see the creator hierarchy (notice the createAndValidateVehicle method now takes a String parameter). (As usual, this parameter could also be represented as an enum to provide stronger type-safety and improve clarity.) Here are the key changes in bold:

// VehicleFactory.java

```java
package appa.demo1.creator;

import factory.vehicles.Vehicle;

public abstract class VehicleFactory
{
    public Vehicle createAndValidateVehicle(String type)
    {
        Vehicle vehicle= createVehicle(type);
        vehicle.validate();
        return vehicle;
    }

    // This is the "factory method".
    protected abstract Vehicle createVehicle(String type);
}
```

Now, look at the concrete factories, **CarFactory** and **MotorcycleFactory**, which interpret the type parameter:

// CarFactory.java

```java
package appa.demo1.creator;

import appa.demo1.product.RegularCar;
import appa.demo1.product.SportsCar;
import factory.vehicles.Vehicle;
```

```java
public class CarFactory extends VehicleFactory {
  @Override
  protected Vehicle createVehicle(String type) {
  Vehicle vehicle = null;
  if (type.equals("regular")) {
    vehicle = new RegularCar();
  } else if (type.equals("sports")) {
    vehicle = new SportsCar();
  } else {
    throw new IllegalArgumentException("Invalid argument: " + type);
  }
  return vehicle;
 }
}

// MotorcycleFactory.java

package appa.demo1.creator;

import appa.demo1.product.RegularMotorcycle;
import appa.demo1.product.SportsMotorcycle;
import factory.vehicles.Vehicle;

public class MotorcycleFactory extends VehicleFactory {
  @Override
  protected Vehicle createVehicle(String type) {
    Vehicle vehicle = null;
    if (type.equals("regular")) {
      vehicle = new RegularMotorcycle();
    } else if (type.equals("sports")) {
    vehicle = new SportsMotorcycle();
    } else {
      throw new IllegalArgumentException("Invalid argument: " + type);
    }
```

```
    return vehicle;
  }
}
```

Now see a sample product:

```java
// RegularCar.java
package appa.demo1.product;

import factory.vehicles.Vehicle;

public class RegularCar extends Vehicle {
  public RegularCar() {
    type = "regular car";
  }
}
```

Note   You can see that I have reused the Vehicle class from the factory.vehicles package. Since the other products (RegularMotorcycle, SportsCar, and SportsMotorcycle) are similar, I do not show them here. You can find these products in the appa.demo1. product package. You can download the complete code (stored in the appa.demo1 package) from the Apress website.

Here is the client code:

```java
// FPDemo4Client.java

package appa.demo1.client;

import appa.demo1.creator.MotorcycleFactory;
import appa.demo1.creator.CarFactory;
import appa.demo1.creator.VehicleFactory;
import factory.vehicles.Vehicle;
```

```java
class FPDemo4Client {
  public static void main(String[] args) {
    System.out.println("The parameterized factory method demonstration.\n");
    VehicleFactory factory= new CarFactory();
    Vehicle vehicle = factory.createAndValidateVehicle("regular");
    System.out.println("Your " + vehicle + " is now ready.");
    System.out.println("-----------");
    vehicle = factory.createAndValidateVehicle("sports");
    System.out.println("Your " + vehicle + " is now ready.");

    System.out.println("\n===================");

    factory = new MotorcycleFactory();
    vehicle = factory.createAndValidateVehicle("regular");
    System.out.println("Your " + vehicle + " is now ready.");
    System.out.println("-----------");
    vehicle = factory.createAndValidateVehicle("sports");
    System.out.println("Your " + vehicle + " is now ready.");
  }
}
```

Output

Upon executing this program, you'll notice the following output:

The parameterized factory method demonstration.

The regular car validation is completed.
Your regular car is now ready.

The sports car validation is completed.
Your sports car is now ready.

===================
The regular motorcycle validation is completed.

Your regular motorcycle is now ready.

The sports motorcycle validation is completed.
Your sports motorcycle is now ready.

Analysis

Notice that in this implementation, though the VehicleFactory obeys the OCP, the concrete factories (CarFactory and MotorcycleFactory) do not follow the OCP. **However, this implementation is more flexible compared to the previous demonstration (Demonstration 3 of Chapter 1).**

In short, if you avoid passing a type parameter and use a dedicated factory class for each subtype, you move closer to strict OCP compliance, but it may also cause a class explosion. However, I focused more on the design flexibilities here. Also, the guidelines of the GoF book allow me to choose a parameterized factory method, and I am OK with that.

In the upcoming demonstration, you'll see an alternative way to balance flexibility and OCP.

Registry-Based Factory

In some implementations, you may find a variation known as a **registry-based factory.** Instead of relying on conditional logic inside the factory (as in the parameterized version), this approach uses a registration mechanism. Let's see it.

Demonstration 2

In this demonstration, the createAndValidateVehicle(String key) method internally calls creator.get(). By calling the get() method, I'll invoke the constructor referenced by the supplier (**which will be shown in the client code shortly**), producing a fresh instance on demand. This ensures that the factory **creates objects dynamically**, rather than storing pre-created instances, preserving the purpose of the Factory pattern.

Here is the new look of the VehicleFactory class:

```java
package appa.demo2;

import java.util.HashMap;
import java.util.Map;
import java.util.function.Supplier;
import factory.vehicles.Vehicle;

public class VehicleFactory {

  private final Map<String, Supplier<Vehicle>> vehicles = new HashMap<>();
  // Register product types
  public void addVehicle(String key, Supplier<Vehicle> creator) {
    vehicles.put(key, creator);
  }

  // Create a product by key
  public Vehicle createAndValidateVehicle(String key) {
    Supplier<Vehicle> creator = vehicles.get(key);
    if (creator == null) {
      throw new IllegalArgumentException("No such vehicle type registered: " + key);
  }
  Vehicle vehicle = creator.get();
  vehicle.validate();
  return vehicle;
  }
}
```

A client can now register products against their constructors as follows:

```java
// Register vehicle types
factory.addVehicle("regular_car", RegularCar::new);
factory.addVehicle("regular_motor", RegularMotorcycle::new);
factory.addVehicle("sports_car", SportsCar::new);
factory.addVehicle("sports_motor", SportsMotorcycle::new);
```

POINT TO NOTE

The following lines are equivalent (see the changes in bold):

factory.addVehicle("regular_car", **RegularCar::new**);

factory.addVehicle("regular_car", **() -> new RegularCar()**);

What is the benefit? Notice that the factory is fully compliant with the OCP now. A client can add a new vehicle type simply by registering, and it does not require any change in the factory code. Let's see a sample client code:

```java
package appa.demo2.client;

import appa.demo1.product.RegularCar;
import appa.demo1.product.RegularMotorcycle;
import appa.demo1.product.SportsCar;
import appa.demo1.product.SportsMotorcycle;
import appa.demo2.VehicleFactory;
import factory.vehicles.Vehicle;

class FPDemo5Client {
  public static void main(String[] args) {
    System.out.println("The registry-based factory demonstration.\n");
    VehicleFactory factory = new VehicleFactory();

    // Register vehicle types
    factory.addVehicle("regular_car", RegularCar::new);
    factory.addVehicle("regular_motor", RegularMotorcycle::new);
    factory.addVehicle("sports_car", SportsCar::new);
    factory.addVehicle("sports_motor", SportsMotorcycle::new);

    // Create vehicles dynamically
    Vehicle vehicle = factory.createAndValidateVehicle("regular_car");
```

```java
        System.out.println("Your " + vehicle + " is now ready.");
        System.out.println("-----------");

        vehicle = factory.createAndValidateVehicle("regular_motor");
        System.out.println("Your " + vehicle + " is now ready.");
        System.out.println("\n===================");

        vehicle = factory.createAndValidateVehicle("sports_car");
        System.out.println("Your " + vehicle + " is now ready.");
        System.out.println("-----------");

        vehicle = factory.createAndValidateVehicle("sports_motor");
        System.out.println("Your " + vehicle + " is now ready.");
    }
}
```

Output

Upon executing this program, you'll notice the following output:

The registry-based factory demonstration.

The regular car validation is completed.
Your regular car is now ready.

The regular motorcycle validation is completed.
Your regular motorcycle is now ready.

===================
The sports car validation is completed.
Your sports car is now ready.

The sports motorcycle validation is completed.
Your sports motorcycle is now ready.

Analysis

You can see that there is no change in the output except for the first line. It follows OCP and is very flexible. However, there is a downside as well. An invalid key can throw a runtime exception (unlike compile-time safety in dedicated factories).

Author's note: While the registry-based factory follows OCP, the client code must still perform the registration of new types. This means the client side is **not fully closed to modification**. However, this trade-off is generally acceptable because it keeps the factory flexible and maintainable, allowing new products to be added without touching the factory implementation itself.

Simplified Implementation

If you would like to avoid the registration process in the client code, you can do so by sacrificing the OCP compliance again. How? Let's analyze the following implementation.

Demonstration 3

You can use a factory that registers all the products in a static block. Here is an example:

```
package appa.demo3;

import java.util.HashMap;
import java.util.Map;
import java.util.function.Supplier;
import appa.demo1.product.RegularCar;
import appa.demo1.product.RegularMotorcycle;
import appa.demo1.product.SportsCar;
import appa.demo1.product.SportsMotorcycle;
import factory.vehicles.Vehicle;
```

```java
public class VehicleFactory {

  private final static Map<String, Supplier<Vehicle>> vehicles = new HashMap<>();
    static {
      vehicles.put("regular_car", RegularCar::new);
      vehicles.put("regular_motor", RegularMotorcycle::new);
      vehicles.put("sports_car", SportsCar::new);
      vehicles.put("sports_motor", SportsMotorcycle::new);
    }

  // Create a product by key
  public Vehicle createAndValidateVehicle(String key) {
      Supplier<Vehicle> creator = vehicles.get(key);
      if (creator == null) {
        throw new IllegalArgumentException("No such vehicle type registered: " + key);
      }
      Vehicle vehicle = creator.get();
      vehicle.validate();
      return vehicle;
    }
}
```

Since this version brings back the issue with OCP compliance, I am not showing you the complete demonstration. However, you can download the full implementation with the client code from the Apress website (see appa. demo3 package).

Final Thoughts

I have shown you six different demonstrations to help you understand the factory patterns. I hope that it's pretty clear to you now. Before you finish reading, I'd like to share my final thoughts as follows:

Using if-else in a concrete factory does not invalidate the Factory Method pattern. The GoF cares about delegating object creation to subclasses, not necessarily strict OCP compliance. OCP is a **guideline for improving maintainability**, which is why the registry pattern is suggested as an enhancement.

Revisiting the Builder Pattern

If you execute Demonstration 3 (or any other demonstration) of Chapter 3, you'll see the following output:

```
*** Builder Pattern Demonstration.***

The car details:
 type=Regular,
 seats=5,
 motor=internal combustion engine (fueled by diesel),
 exhaustEmissionSystem=true
============
The car details:
 type=Electric,
 seats=4,
 motor=electric motors and batteries,
 exhaustEmissionSystem=false
============
```

Exercise

This is fine. However, displaying the construction sequence can beautify the implementation. **Can you refactor any of these demonstrations (say Demonstration 3) to reflect those steps?** Here is a sample output for your reference:

*** Builder Pattern Demonstration.***

The car is constructed as follows:
The body of a regular car is made.
The internal combustion engine (fueled by diesel) is set.
Adjusted 5 seats in the car.
An exhaust emission system is set.

============

The car is constructed as follows:
The body of an electric car is made.
Adjusted 4 seats in the car.
The electric motors and batteries are set.

============

You may solve this exercise in various ways. **I keep this exercise for you.**

Author's note: I can give you a clue: you can use a suitable data structure to store the construction sequence.

Key

You can find a sample solution inside the builder.demo4 package.

In this implementation, I used a LinkedList to store these construction steps. However, if you want to ensure that no step is accidentally recorded more than once, using a LinkedHashSet would be a safer alternative. It preserves insertion order while enforcing the Set contract, thereby preventing duplicates. As a subclass of HashSet, it offers both uniqueness and deterministic iteration order.

Revisiting the Prototype Pattern

Chapter 4 discussed the Prototype pattern. It started with a simple demonstration (Demonstration 1) where the client directly creates an initial object and clones it using the clone() method. There, I talked about deep copying, compared with shallow copying, and compared the techniques by analyzing the effects of some updates on the cloned object.

REMINDER

I have also included an alternative version of this demonstration that uses a copy constructor rather than the clone() method. You can find it in the prototype.demo1.alt package.

Demonstration 2 continued the discussion by centralizing prototype management in a CarFactory, allowing clients to obtain clones without knowing the concrete classes. It also used the Cloneable approach for deep copying. **However, writing manual clone() methods for multiple objects can be tedious and error-prone, especially when the object graph is complex.** An alternative is to use an external library for cloning. Let me show you another demonstration that also conveys the idea of the Prototype pattern now.

Author's note: A deep copy mechanism copies the root object and all objects reachable from it. However, a shallow copy mechanism copies the root object only.

Using an External Library (Apache Commons Lang)

You can use Apache Commons Lang's SerializationUtils.clone() to perform deep copies in a single line, reduce boilerplate, and optionally reset fields after cloning.

REMINDER

The fields of the Model class are declared as public solely to keep this Prototype pattern example simple and focused. As mentioned earlier in Chapter 4, in production code, these would typically be private with appropriate getters and setters.

Demonstration 4

Here is the Model class with the key changes in bold:

```java
// Model.java

package appa.demo4;

import java.io.Serializable;

public class Model implements Serializable{
  public String modelName;
  public String color;
  public Model(String modelName, String color) {
   this.modelName = modelName;
   this.color = color;
  }
  @Override
  public String toString() {
   return modelName + ", Color:" + color;
  }
}
```

Here is the Car class with the key changes in bold:

```java
// Car.java (Abstract prototype)

package appa.demo4;

import java.io.Serializable;

public abstract class Car implements Serializable {
  protected Model model;
  protected double price;
  public Car(Model model, double price) {
    this.model = model;
    this.price = price;
  }

  // No need to override the clone method anymore

  protected void resetModelAndPrice() {
    // Resetting the model
    this.model = new Model("Not defined", "Not set");
    // Resetting the price as well
    this.price = 0;
  }
  public abstract void updateCar(String modelName, String color, double price);
}
```

Before you see the Ford class, let me highlight a few points:

- Since the Car class (the parent class of Ford) already implements the Serializable interface, you do not write something like: class Ford extends Car implements Serializable { ..}. Instead, class Ford extends Car { ..} should be enough.

- In Demonstration 2 of Chapter 4, the Ford class had the package-private visibility. So, the client could not use it directly. Instead, the client needed to use the CarFactory class to get a Ford car. For the same reason, the Ford class is not public here as well.

- Since the Car class and the Model class reside in the same package appa.demo4, you do not see the import statements for those classes in the following file (Ford.java).

Let's see the Ford class now:

```java
// Ford.java

package appa.demo4;

// Restricting the visibility of the Ford class. It is not public here.
// Since its parent class already implements the Serializable interface,
// extending the Car class should be enough.

// import java.io.Serializable; // Not required here
// class Ford extends Car implements Serializable { // Not required here

class Ford extends Car {
  private String company;
  public Ford(Model model, double price) {
    super(model, price);
    company = "Ford";
  }
  @Override
  public void updateCar(String modelName, String color, double price) {
    this.model.modelName=modelName;
    this.model.color=color;
    this.price = price;
  }
```

```java
  @Override
  public String toString() {
    return "Company:" + company + ", Model: " + model + ", Price:" + price + "\n";
  }
}
```

Here is the CarFactory class with the key changes in bold:

```java
// CarFactory.java

package appa.demo4;

import java.util.Map;
import java.util.HashMap;
import java.io.Serializable;
import org.apache.commons.lang3.SerializationUtils;

public class CarFactory implements Serializable {
  public static Map<String, Car> prototypes = new HashMap<>();
  static {
    // Will clone from a Maverick Ford car
    prototypes.put("ford", new Ford(new Model("Maverick", "Silver"), 25000));
    // Add other prototypes if any
  }
  public static Car getPrototypeOf(String car) {
    Car prototype = prototypes.get(car);
    if (prototype == null) {
      throw new IllegalArgumentException("Unknown car type: " + car);
    }
    // Utility one-liner deep copy
    Car clonedCar = SerializationUtils.clone(prototype);
    // Reset model and price
```

```java
    clonedCar.resetModelAndPrice();
    return clonedCar;
  }
}
```

It's time to see a sample client code, which is as follows:

```java
// ThirdPartyPrototypeDemoClient.java (Client)

package appa.demo4.client;

import appa.demo4.Car;
import appa.demo4.CarFactory;

class ThirdPartyPrototypeDemoClient {
  public static void main(String[] args) {
    System.out.println("***Prototype Pattern Demo-3***\n");
    System.out.println("Getting a Ford car with some default settings by cloning.");
    Car clonedCar = CarFactory.getPrototypeOf("ford");
    System.out.println(clonedCar);
    System.out.println("=============================");

    System.out.println("Updating the model and price of the cloned car now.");
    clonedCar.updateCar("Ranger", "Blue",40000);
    System.out.println("After update, here are the new car details:");
    System.out.println(clonedCar);
    System.out.println("=============================");

    System.out.println("Getting another Ford car with some default settings by cloning.");
    Car clonedCar2 = CarFactory.getPrototypeOf("ford"); // If reset is required
    System.out.println(clonedCar2);
  }
}
```

Author's note: You may see some warnings about serialVersionUID in Eclipse. Here is a sample: *The serializable class Car does not declare a static final serialVersionUID field of type long.* You can ignore warnings for short-lived demo objects. However, it's recommended to define it in production code for all Serializable classes.

Additional tip: Eclipse offers a **"quick fix"** (just move your cursor on the class name or press Ctrl+1) to resolve this warning. For example, you can get options like "Add default serialization version ID," "Add generated serialization version ID," or "Suppress the warning." You can choose an option depending on your needs.

Output

Upon executing this program, you'll notice the following output:

```
***Prototype Pattern Demo-3***

Getting a Ford car with some default settings by cloning.
Company:Ford, Model: Not defined, Color:Not set, Price:0.0


==============================
Updating the model and price of the cloned car now.
After update, here are the new car details:
Company:Ford, Model: Ranger, Color:Blue, Price:40000.0


==============================
Getting another Ford car with some default settings by cloning.
Company:Ford, Model: Not defined, Color:Not set, Price:0.0
```

You have seen the same output except the first line in Demonstration 2 of Chapter 4 as well. Now, let us add a utility method in the CarFactory as follows:

```java
public class CarFactory implements Serializable {

    // There is no change in the previous code that you saw earlier

    // Optional method- added for flexibility to choose the reset option
    public static Car getPrototypeOf(String car, boolean reset) {
      Car prototype = prototypes.get(car);
      if (prototype == null) {
        throw new IllegalArgumentException("Unknown car type: " + car);
      }
      // Utility one-liner deep copy
      Car clonedCar = SerializationUtils.clone(prototype);
      // Reset model and price if required
      if (reset) {
        clonedCar.resetModelAndPrice();
      }
      return clonedCar;
      }
}
```

Let's modify a line in the client code as shown below:

```java
class ThirdPartyPrototypeDemoClient {
    public static void main(String[] args) {
        // There is  no change in the previous code
        System.out.println("Getting another Ford car with some default settings by cloning.");
        // If reset is not required
        Car clonedCar2 = CarFactory.getPrototypeOf("ford",false);
        System.out.println(clonedCar2);
    }
}
```

Upon executing the program, this time, you'll see the following output (notice the change in the last line of the output):

```
***Prototype Pattern Demo-3***

Getting a Ford car with some default settings by cloning.
Company:Ford, Model: Not defined, Color:Not set, Price:0.0


==============================
Updating the model and price of the cloned car now.
After update, here are the new car details:
Company:Ford, Model: Ranger, Color:Blue, Price:40000.0


==============================
Getting another Ford car with some default settings by cloning.
Company:Ford, Model: Maverick, Color:Silver, Price:25000.0
```

You have explored classical creational design patterns in the first five chapters of this book. This appendix shows that the patterns can be **extended, enhanced, and adapted** to solve more real-world problems. From the flexibility of parameterized factories to the maintainability of registry-based factories and from the sequence-aware Builder pattern (covered as an exercise, with a sample implementation available for download from the Apress website) to practical Prototype cloning, you now have a richer toolkit for designing robust, reusable, and scalable code.

What's Next?

This book covered five useful creational design patterns with many examples. By now, I hope you have a solid understanding of these patterns. The natural next step is to **apply them in your own programs, keep experimenting with new code, and learn continuously**—because, as we all know, practice makes perfect.

I also encourage you to explore related topics from other books, articles, or blogs. However, don't forget the classic **GoF book** listed below. Though it was published decades ago, you'll find it highly relevant even in 2026—this is why it remains a bestseller on Amazon!

Remember that programming languages often provide features that make certain patterns easier to implement, but **design patterns themselves are not tied to any specific language**. So keep studying, practicing, and revisiting these ideas in your projects.

The next step is to learn from other books or articles, exercise these patterns in your programs, and keep experimenting with new code. I, too, keep experimenting with patterns and have written several books on design patterns using C# and Java. For example, *Java Design Patterns 3rd Edition* (Apress, 2022) and *Design Patterns in C# Second Edition* (Apress, 2020) covered all 23 GoF patterns and some additional patterns. They also discussed anti-patterns and commonly asked questions on design patterns. One of my recent books, *Parallel Programming with C# and .NET*, discussed Task-based Asynchronous Pattern (TAP) and related topics. If interested, you can learn those patterns from these books as well.

© Vaskaran Sarcar 2026
V. Sarcar, *Creational Design Patterns in Java*, Apress Pocket Guides,
https://doi.org/10.1007/979-8-8688-2314-5

In the following list, you will also see a few more books from which I got many new insights during my exploration of design patterns. Though Java is now enriched with many new and powerful features, I still believe that these books (or their updated editions) can be equally effective for you.

Books

Here is my recommended list of books for you.

- *Design Patterns: Elements of Reusable Object-Oriented Software* by Erich Gamma et al. (Addison-Wesley, 1994)

- *Java Design Patterns* by Vaskaran Sarcar, Third Edition (Apress, 2022)

- *Head First Design Patterns* by Eric Freeman and Elisabeth Robson, Second Edition (O'Reilly Media, 2021)

- *Java Design Pattern Essentials* by Tony Bevis, Second Edition (Ability First Limited, 2012)

- *Design Patterns For Dummies* by Steve Holzner (Wiley Publishing, Inc., 2006)

Other Resources

In today's world, online platforms are very powerful. For example, you can always learn from Google, Stack Overflow, Quora, YouTube, LinkedIn Learning, or Udemy. You can use these online platforms to learn not only design patterns but almost anything you want. However, you must validate the content.

In addition, in each chapter, I referred to some links in our discussions and Q&A Sessions. You can have a detailed look at those links to learn more.

Final Note

As you continue exploring other patterns in this book, keep experimenting, and continue to think about trade-offs, OCP compliance, and practical usage scenarios to make your application flexible as well as maintainable. I wish you the best of luck!

Other Books by the Author

The following list includes other Apress books written by the author:

- *Delegates, Events, and Lambda Expressions in C#* (Apress, 2025)

- *Python Bootcamp* (Apress, 2025)

- *Creational Design Patterns in C#* (Apress, 2025)

- *Task Programming in C# and .NET* (Apress, 2025)

- *Parallel Programming with C# and .NET* (Apress, 2024)

- *Introducing Functional Programming Using C#* (Apress, 2023)

- *Simple and Efficient Programming in C# Second Edition* (Apress, 2022)

- *Test Your Skills in C# Programming* (Apress, 2022)

- *Java Design Patterns Third Edition* (Apress, 2022)

- *Simple and Efficient Programming in C#* (Apress, 2021)

- *Design Patterns in C# Second Edition* (Apress, 2020)

- *Getting Started with Advanced C#* (Apress, 2020)

V. Sarcar, *Creational Design Patterns in Java*, Apress Pocket Guides,
https://doi.org/10.1007/979-8-8688-2314-5

- *Interactive Object-Oriented Programming in Java Second Edition* (Apress, 2019)

- *Java Design Patterns Second Edition* (Apress, 2019)

- *Design Patterns in C#* (Apress, 2018)

- *Interactive C#* (Apress, 2017)

- *Interactive Object-Oriented Programming in Java* (Apress, 2016)

- *Java Design Patterns* (Apress, 2016)

The following list includes his non-Apress books:

- *Python Bookcamp* (Amazon, 2021)

- *Operating System: Computer Science Interview Series* (CreateSpace, 2014)

To explore these books, you can visit any of the following links:

- https://amazon.com/author/vaskaran_sarcar

- https://link.springer.com/search?newsearch=true&query=vaskar an+sarcar&content-type=book&dateFrom=&dateTo=&sortBy=ne westFirst

GPSR Compliance
The European Union's (EU) General Product Safety Regulation (GPSR) is a set
of rules that requires consumer products to be safe and our obligations to
ensure this.

If you have any concerns about our products, you can contact us on

ProductSafety@springernature.com

In case Publisher is established outside the EU, the EU authorized
representative is:

Springer Nature Customer Service Center GmbH
Europaplatz 3
69115 Heidelberg, Germany